TWAYNE'S WORLD AUTHORS SERIES

A Survey of the World's Literature

Sylvia E. Bowman, Indiana University

GENERAL EDITOR

SPAIN AND PORTUGAL

Gerald E. Wade, Vanderbilt University

EDITOR

Gil Vicente

(*TWAS 29*)

TWAYNE'S WORLD AUTHORS SERIES (TWAS)

The purpose of TWAS is to survey the major writers —novelists, dramatists, historians, poets, philosophers, and critics—of the nations of the world. Among the national literatures covered are those of Australia, Canada, China, Eastern Europe, France, Germany, Greece, India, Italy, Japan, Latin America, New Zealand, Poland, Russia, Scandinavia, Spain, and the African nations, as well as Hebrew, Yiddish, and Latin Classical literatures. This survey is complemented by Twayne's United States Authors Series and English Authors Series

The intent of each volume in these series is to present a critical-analytical study of the works of the writer; to include biographical and historical material that may be necessary for understanding, appreciation, and critical appraisal of the writer; and to present all material in clear, concise English—but not to vitiate the scholarly content of the work by doing so.

Gil Vicente

By JACK HORACE PARKER

University of Toronto

Twayne Publishers, Inc.   ::   New York

To My Wife

Preface

"It is not very easy," wrote José Almeida Pavão in 1963, "to be original at the present time, when one is trying to speak of Gil Vicente, in view of the fact that the critics have dealt with him under so many and so varied facets." [1] Yet, the celebration, in 1965, of the five-hundredth anniversary of the dramatist's birth, was accompanied by a large number of studies, some of amazing originality; and Reis Brasil was able to make the following significant statement: "We are convinced that there exists a great avidity for all that refers to Gil Vicente, for everything that concerns his works and their projection in national culture, in Peninsular culture, and in European and World culture." [2]

In view of this declared and proven interest, it seems hardly amiss, therefore, to add one more item to the already vast bibliography of a dramatic poet of world significance, who stands at the end of the Middle Ages. One who has the honor of belonging to two great literatures: that of Portugal and that of Spain.* A brief monograph in English which attempts to assess his literary activity and his place in the history of theater will, it is hoped, have some place of value, and will make this Portuguese-Spanish "Shakespeare" better known to English-speaking readers.

Both the chronology and the classification of Gil Vicente's works are very uncertain. Likewise, there is a total lack of documentation concerning the childhood and youth of this important literary figure. Even details concerning his adult years are very few. What we do have are the works themselves, thanks to the

---

* Since Gil Vicente wrote in both Portuguese and Spanish, the spelling of certain words which appear throughout this book depends on the language in which they are written. The most common of these are: Dom Duardos, Don Duardos; Amadis de Gaula, Amadís de Gaula; Garcia, García; Maria, María; etc.

compilation of his complete (or almost complete) works by his son Luis (the *Copilação* of 1562). These works can be carefully studied in the attempt to evaluate the literary worth of this dramatist who, as the eminent Spanish critic Marcelino Menéndez Pelayo put it at the end of the nineteenth century, had no rival to surpass him in the Europe of his time.

The chronology which is followed in this volume is often tentative, but it is based on sound critics such as Anselmo Braamcamp Freire and Aubrey Fitz Gerald Bell. The classification or grouping of the plays followed here (which is my own) is somewhat arbitrary. It has followed a division which seems to evolve very naturally: from the Spanish *début* (plays growing out of the influence of the Salamancan masters) through the continuation of this Salamancan tradition, which was not entirely lost in later years; to the Moralities and Mysteries, which were a high point in the Vicentine art; and back to the beginning of and the development of the vast number of plays which can be classified roughly as "farces" and "comedies" (with a whole chapter devoted to the chivalrous *Dom Duardos* and *Amadis de Gaula*). And, since Gil Vicente left a few compositions other than theater, there is a chapter devoted to his miscellaneous works in verse and in prose. Other systems of classification might very well have been adopted, for it is very true that various critics have had their individual preferences, and the *Copilação* of 1562 had its own groupings too; but none of these groupings or divisions so far suggested is entirely satisfactory.[3]

Since Gil Vicente stands out as a lyric dramatic poet, and as a dramatic lyric poet, in his function as Impresario of the Portuguese Court, it has been felt of value to devote a chapter to his special lyric achievements in his "songs," and one to his activities in Court entertainment. No court of Europe was so fortunate at the time, in those first years of the sixteenth century, as the Portuguese Court, which had a man of such varied talents to whom to entrust its many celebrations and commemorations.

In view of the richness of Vicentine bibliography—the large volume produced by Lisbon's Biblioteca Nacional in 1942 is witness to the many writings on the author up to that time[4]—the references have had to be selected with the greatest of care. The selection has been made with attention to the English-reading

Preface

public as far as possible, but it has been very necessary to include a considerable body of pertinent material in foreign languages. The specialist will find many desirable items wanting, but he will be guided through what is presented to the riches of the field. If this volume can be considered to be an introduction to a man who is really worth while knowing, the author's purpose will be achieved.

J. H. PARKER

University of Toronto

Acknowledgments

Special acknowledgment is made to the Humanities and Social Sciences Committee of the Office of Research Administration, University of Toronto, for Grants in Aid of Research for this study of Gil Vicente. Funds provided by the Office have permitted visits to libraries in the United States and in Europe. The appreciation of the author is likewise expressed to Mrs. T. B. Barclay, M.A., who carefully typed the manuscript for the printer.

Contents

Preface

Chronology

1. The Dramatist-Goldsmith 17
2. The Spanish *Début* 29
3. The Continuation of the Salamancan Tradition 36
4. The Moralities and the Mysteries 54
5. The Farces and the Comedies 73
6. The Plays of Chivalry 99
7. The Miscellaneous Works 108
8. Gil Vicente's Songs 122
9. Gil Vicente the Impresario 133
10. Limitations and Achievements 144

Notes and References 151

Selected Bibliography 161

Index 165

Chronology

1465   Gil Vicente born about this date, in a rural district of Portugal.

1490   Festivities in Evora to celebrate the wedding of Crown Prince Afonso and Princess Isabel of Castile may have drawn Gil Vicente, the goldsmith, to Court.

1490   About this year, Gil Vicente married Branca Bezerra.

1495   João II died, and his widow's brother, Manuel I, ascended the throne.

1502   Gil Vicente began his dramatic career with *The Herdsman's Monologue,* to honor the Spanish Queen Maria on the occasion of the birth of an heir to the throne (later João III).

1502–   Plays for Christmas and Epiphany, for the dowager Queen
1503   Leanor, were written and presented.

1506   The famous Belém monstrance, preserved today in Lisbon's Museum of Ancient Art, was completed from gold tribute from the Far East.

1508   Vicente's *début* in farce took place with *Who Has Bran?*.

1509   Appointed overseer of the gold and silver artifacts in Lisbon, Tomar, and elsewhere.

1513   Became Master of the Royal Mint and a member of the Lisbon Town Council.

1514   Gil Vicente's first wife died about this time.

1516–   The excellent Morality Plays, *The Soul's Journey* and *The*
1519   *Ships,* were written and presented.

1517   The probable date of Gil Vicente's second marriage, to Melícia Rodrigues.

1519   The probable date of the birth of Gil Vicente's elder daughter, Paula.

1520   The probable date of the birth of Gil Vicente's son, Luis.

1521   In August, *The Courts of Jupiter* was performed to wish "bon voyage" to Princess Isabel, who was leaving to marry the Duke of Savoy.

1521   In December, King Manuel died and João III was crowned.

1522   Vicente composed the interesting dramatic poem, *Maria Parda's Lament*, a reflection of the lack of foodstuffs and wine.

1522–   The Plays of Chivalry, *Dom Duardos* and *Amadis de*
1523   *Gaula,* can be assigned to these years.

1523   The famous *Farce of Inês Pereira* was performed before the King in the Monastery of the Knights of Christ, in Tomar.

1524   *The Forge of Love* was presented at Evora to celebrate João III's betrothal to Princess Catarina of Castile.

1524   Gil Vicente received two small pensions from the King.

1525   Death of the dowager Queen Leanor, widow of João II, and patroness of Gil Vicente.

1526–   Gil Vicente was especially busy in these years with theatri-
1527   cals for the Court.

1527   *The Ship of Love* was written for Queen Catarina's entry into Lisbon.

1528   Gil Vicente received a further pension from João III.

1529   *The Triumph of Winter* celebrated the birth of Princess Isabel.

1531   Gil Vicente preached a sermon to the friars of Santarém on the subject of tolerance.

1533   *The Pilgrimage of the Aggrieved* was performed to celebrate the birth of Prince Felipe.

1535   Prince Denis was born, and it is a novelty that Gil Vicente seems not to have composed a play for the occasion!

1536   A Papal Bull established the Inquisition in Portugal.

1536   Gil Vicente's last play, *The Forest of Deceits,* was performed at Evora.

1536   This is the probable year of Gil Vicente's composition of his epistle-dedication of his Works to João III.

1537   The probable year of Gil Vicente's death.

1562   The important compilation of Gil Vicente's complete works (the *Copilação*) was printed in Lisbon by his son Luis.

CHAPTER 1

The Dramatist-Goldsmith

I *Gil Vicente's Life*

GIL VICENTE was born about the year 1465. His *Festival Play (Auto da Festa)* of ca. 1525 speaks of its author by name as being "big-bellied and over sixty," and from this data, through a simple mathematical subtraction, the year 1465 is reached.[1] This date has been accepted by most historians of the Portuguese theater, and Vicente's native land chose, positively, the year 1965 to celebrate the five-hundredth anniversary of the playwright's birth.

Several towns or regions of Portugal have claimed the honor of being Gil Vicente's place of birth. Barcelos, Guimarães, Lisbon, the province of Beira—all these and many more have aspired to the glory of having fathered such a distinguished son. Not too long ago, Guimarães, in the North, which was indeed the birthplace of Portugal's first king, Afonso Henriques, of the twelfth century, laid strong claim to this distinction through a monograph by António Lopes de Carvalho,[2] which points to earlier genealogical studies by the Visconde de Sanches de Baena,[3] and to the presence of Guimarães "culture" (words, phrases, customs) in the plays. Against this claim to fame by Guimarães, several critics are inclined to favor Beira, for the plays reveal a very special knowledge of this province, with many references to Beira settings and much use of Beira dialect. This opinion, first advanced in a vigorous fashion by José Leite de Vasconcelos,[4] has been accepted only tentatively by Aubrey Fitz Gerald Bell, known for his many splendid studies of the dramatist.[5] Bell, with Anselmo Braamcamp Freire, in his definitive *Life*,[6] although inclined to accept Guimarães, only concludes that Gil Vicente was certainly country-born and raised. The pastoral quality of his plays exhibits much too intimate an acquaintanceship with rural life to permit the belief that he was a city man, who came, let us say, from Lisbon.

Very recently, Amândio Marques, by references to several plays, has put forth arguments for Guimarães de Tavares, a town in the Beira Alta.[7] While it is still impossible to pinpoint Gil Vicente's place of origin, it seems not unlikely that some locale, in or near the Serra da Estrêla (Beira Alta), which he speaks of so frequently, is to be favored.

Similarly, Gil Vicente's education, or lack of it, has provoked much controversy. If we are to honor Bell's frequently expressed opinion, it seems evident that Vicente's knowledge of literary materials was a very superficial one. Carolina Michaëlis de Vasconcelos, a critic of note, had the same idea, when she rejected the statement made by some that Gil Vicente was a reader of Latin classics and of the humanists of the Renaissance.[8] Not too long ago, however, Joaquim de Carvalho argued that Gil Vicente must have read widely in patristic literature, and even suggested that the dramatist might have studied at a university in Portugal, in Spain, or in France.[9] Following that, the Bell-Michaëlis de Vasconcelos opinion was strongly defended, and the Carvalho idea completely rejected, by I. S. Révah;[10] with Révah insisting that Gil Vicente's learning, as revealed in his writings, arose from knowledge of the day, common to all, from books of devotion in Spanish and in Portuguese, and from Gil Vicente's activities as a goldsmith, well versed in religious iconography of the times.

Extensive perusal of the Vicentine writings inclines us to the side of Révah's arguments, which immediately bring to mind the storm of controversy which has raged over the years as to whether Gil Vicente, the dramatist, and Gil Vicente, the goldsmith, were one and the same man. Official, contemporary documents make reference to a "Gil Vicente, goldsmith to the dowager Queen Leanor," the queen who was the dramatist's patroness; and Teófilo Braga, in several critical writings of the end of the nineteenth century and beginning of the twentieth century, came to the conclusion that they were two different men—cousins.[11] By 1907, however, in an article in the *Jornal do Comércio*, Anselmo Braamcamp Freire entered into the verbal fray to insist, as he continued to insist until his death, that there was only one Gil Vicente, the poet-goldsmith; or as he put it in the title to his biography: "Gil Vicente, Troubador and Master of the Royal Mint."

In modern times, the only serious disagreement with the acceptable and probable Braamcamp Freire thesis is to be found in the writings of António José Saraiva.[12] Saraiva's main arguments against the dramatist's and goldsmith's being the same person are (a) the dramatist's begging from time to time for Royal favors and rewards (incompatible, thinks Saraiva, with the attitude of a goldsmith who held important posts in the realm), and (b) the fact that the dramatist's "culture" as revealed in his plays is not that of an artisan.[13] Saraiva's considered arguments are worth noting, it is true. However, I think that they can be overcome, as lacking in any solid proof. And my own conclusion is that the two professions were definitely held by one man. For after all, Braamcamp Freire's rhetorical question is still pertinent: "Is it credible that two men of the same name should exist at the same time, serving the same Queen Leanor, one becoming known in 1502 as a dramatist, the other in 1503 [as a goldsmith], both dying [about] 1539. . . . , and not a word in documents to differentiate them?" (*Vida*, p. 28). In a period when modifiers of "senior," "junior," etc., were used so commonly, the answer to Braamcamp Freire's query is the answer he expected—a vigorous "No!"

Of Gil Vicente the dramatist a great deal will be said in the chapters following. Of Gil Vicente's goldsmith activities, it is sufficient to note that as a young man he may have been apprenticed to the goldsmith's trade, perhaps working with his father or uncle. "It is extremely probable," writes Bell, "that [Gil Vicente] was drawn to the Court, then at Evora, for the first time in 1490 by the unprecedented festivities in honour of the wedding of the Crown Prince and Isabel, daughter of the Catholic Kings, and was one of the many goldsmiths who came thither on the occasion." [14] As the contemporary Garcia de Resende put it in his *Chronicle of King John II*, Chapter 117, "And so the King ordered to come from Castile and other places many goldsmiths to make ornaments and other ornate artifacts." From that time on Gil Vicente's career seems to have been assured, under the patronage of João II, and of his Queen (and later widow) Leanor, who was the sister of João's successor, Manuel I.

By 1506, Gil Vicente had completed the famous monstrance (preserved today in the National Ancient Art Museum in Lisbon) for the Monastery of the Jerónimos at Belém from the first gold brought back from the Far East by Vasco da Gama on his second voyage to India. In 1509, Gil Vicente was appointed overseer of the gold and silver artifacts being wrought for the Hospital of All Saints, Lisbon, for the Monastery of Belém, and for the Monastery of the Order of Christ, in Tomar. In 1512, he was elected one of the Lisbon "Twenty-Four" by the Guild of Goldsmiths, and in 1513, he became Master of the Royal Mint, a post which he held for four and one-half years, while occupying a seat on the Lisbon Town Council.

This Vicentine activity in the goldsmith's trade, and the dramatic activity of the years 1502–1536, were against a background of vast Portuguese achievement. The explorations down the coast of Africa and around the Cape of Good Hope to the Far East (inspired by the spade work of Henry the Navigator, who died in 1460, and his Schools of Navigation and of Shipbuilding at Sagres) occupied the minds of the men of the reign of João II (died in 1495), of Manuel I (died in 1521), and of João III (died in 1557), with only a slight decline in interest by the end of the Vicentine years. Lisbon became the center of commercial and cultural activity, and Gil Vicente, whenever the Court was in residence in that city, had much to observe and reflect upon. Portugal had close connections with all of the leading countries of Europe, and saw its empire expanding and growing in Africa, in Asia, and to some extent in America, for Brazil had been discovered in 1500 by Pedro Alvares Cabral.

King Manuel's reign was a high point in Portuguese history, and the "Manueline style" came to be well known in all branches of artistic endeavor. Henry VIII of England invested Manuel, his brother-in-law, with the Order of the Garter in 1511. The Portuguese embassy to Pope Leo X, in 1514, led by Garcia de Resende, with its magnificent oriental gifts, would be the talk of the Christian world for years. In 1521, for example, a grand reception was held in Lisbon to receive a delegation from Venice, and in the same year, Princess Beatriz departed, after lavish Court celebrations in which Gil Vicente took part, to marry the Duke of Savoy. But by the end of that same year, "the magnificent King Manuel was dead, and his son, the more care-ridden João III, was on the throne." By the mid-twenties, "there was plague and famine in the land. The discovery of a direct route to the East and its apparently inexhaustible wealth had not brought prosperity to the Portuguese provinces. There the chief effect had been to make men discontented with their lot and to lure away even the humblest workers to seek their fortune and often to find death or a far less independent poverty. . . ." "The result," continues Bell (*Four Plays*, p. 78), "was that the old rustic jollity which Vicente had known so well in his youth was dying out, and the very songs of the peasants took on a plaintive air."

Of Gil Vicente's personal life throughout the reigns of Manuel I and João III details are very few. The study of his literary works will show how busy he was, during the years 1502–1536, fulfilling his function as "musician, actor, dramatist, lyric poet" [15] at the Royal Court. Court travels from Lisbon to Almeirim, Coimbra, Evora, Tomar, and other towns (but never out of Portugal), and the many celebrations of royal weddings, births, etc., kept him very occupied indeed; but he did enter into poetic contests, wrote a lament for a deceased sovereign and an ode to acclaim the successor, and "preached" some sermons in verse and in prose on several subjects. He was married twice: for the first time, toward the end of the fifteenth century, to Branca Bezerra, and the eldest son, whose name is uncertain, was born about 1492. A second son, Belchior, was born some years later, and the first wife died around 1514. About 1517, Gil Vicente married Melícia Rodrigues; and a daughter, Paula, who was associated with her father's last theatrical productions, was born ca. 1519. A son, Luis, who played the important rôle of collecting and editing his father's works, to publish the above-mentioned *Copilação* of 1562, was born about 1520. About ten years later, a second daughter, Valéria, came into the world. From time to time, during the "dramatic" years, official documents show that Gil Vicente was the recipient of small awards and pensions, including "clothing allowances," from his two sovereigns, Manuel I and João III, who, generally speaking, seem to have appreciated his services at Court.

The dramatist died not long after the performance of his last play. This *Forest of Deceits* (*Floresta de Enganos*) was performed before the Court in Evora, in December, 1536, and Gil Vicente himself probably took the part of the "Judge" (the *Justiça maior* or *Juiz*). By April, 1540, he was dead, for a reference of that year is to "Belchior Vicente, son of Gil Vicente, whom may God pardon . . ." (the usual pious mention of one departed). The only conclusion that the Lisbon Academy of Sciences could reach in wishing to commemorate the dramatist's anniversary of death was that it would be well to commemorate the finale of his theatrical writings. "Lacking any other precise date," announced Júlio Dantas to the Academy in April, 1936, "this date [December, 1936] can be commemorated. Since the Academy will not be in session in December of this year, it would seem to me to be suitable to consecrate the year 1937 to the systematic study of the person and of the work of Gil Vicente, which today have both assumed an interest not only national, but also universal." [16]

Gil Vicente left for us—at least the *Copilação* assigns it to his pen—his own epitaph:

> I who lie this stone below
> For the Day of Judgment wait,
> From life's weary fevered state
> Resting now.[17]

> (O gram juizo esperando,
> Jaço aqui nesta morada;
> Também da vida cansada
> Descansando.)
> (*Obras completas*, VI, 261)

To these lines, the *Copilação* adds eight additional ones in a similar vein, which lines, however, are not considered to be genuine Vicentine.

II *The Complete Works*

Gil Vicente's Collected Works (the *Copilação*) were published, as has been mentioned, by his son Luis, in 1562. The city of publication was Lisbon, and the patroness of the volume was Dona Catarina, widow of João III, who was acting in the name of the new king, Dom Sebastião. In 1536 the Inquisition had been established in Portugal, and there was strict ecclesiastical censorship. Thanks to the protection of the Queen Mother, however, this first edition escaped any suppressions or deletions, as later printings did not. The second edition of the *Copilação*, of 1586, which was the last for two hundred and fifty years,[18] came forth much mutilated and "corrected"; and I. S. Révah has shown that the Index of

Prohibited Books, from 1551 on, reflects the violent objection to quite a few of the Vicentine plays in which the clergy is portrayed in a bad light and taken to task for its sinful ways.[19] Indeed, concludes Révah, "the *Copilação* of 1562 could not have seen the light of day had it not been for the energetic intervention of Queen Catherine in favor of Gil Vicente's works."

In a recent article, Stephen Reckert points out that there exist six known copies of this important volume: one each in the Universities of Göttingen and Harvard, in the Palace of Mafra, in the Biblioteca Nacional, Lisbon, in the Archives of the Torre do Tombo, Lisbon, and in the Palace of the Braganzas in Vila Viçosa.[20] The National Library of Lisbon put out a facsimile edition in 1928, but Professor Reckert warns that the photocopy, from retouched negatives, renders an erroneous impression of the original, in that several new errors have been introduced and several errors of the original have been "corrected." Reckert, intervening effectively in the question as to whether Luis Vicente altered his father's texts as he prepared them for the printer of 1562, concludes that the printing of the volume was "carried out with a good deal more care than could be suspected to judge only by the facsimile." [21]

Omitted from the *Copilação* for unknown reasons was the previously-mentioned *Auto da Festa,* discovered by the Conde de Sabugosa and published by him in Lisbon, 1906. This play has been accepted without question by the critics as being genuinely Vicentine, and has been included in subsequent printings of the Complete Works. But the critics have not widely accepted, however, as part of the genuine Vicentine canon, two other plays which I. S. Révah has urged upon them. These are *The Play of God the Father, Justice and Mercy* (*Auto de Deus Padre, Justiça e Misericórdia*) and *Human Genesis* (*Obra da Geração Humana*), which Révah presented and discussed in two monographs.[22] Effective arguments against Vicentine authorship have been put forth by Alvaro Júlio da Costa Pimpão[23] and by Paul Teyssier.[24] The former deals with bibliographical data surrounding these two anonymous plays of the sixteenth century and their literary quality, and the latter studies the linguistic characteristics. If the first critic cannot accept the plays as Vicente's for their poverty of style, the second definitely rejects the *Auto de Deus Padre* because it does not include even *one* example of Gil Vicente's constant Leonese palatalization. "This fact," declares Teyssier, "definitely establishes that this play is not by Gil Vicente." But for the *Obra da Geração Humana* the facts, linguistically, are not as clear, but certain linguistic traits do argue against the attribution. "In the absence of positive proofs, we must then reserve judgment," concludes Teyssier, "that is to say, abstain from considering this play as Vicentine." In view of the fact that both plays have far from proven themselves to be Gil Vicente's, my belief is that they are not his, and they are hereby excluded from the discussion of the dramatist's works.

One Vicentine play, no longer extant, which raised a storm of protest on the part of the Church, was *Love's Jubilee* (*Jubileu de Amor*), which was played in Brussels, in the home of the Portuguese Ambassador, Dom Pedro de Mascarenhas, on December 21, 1531. The celebration was in honor of the birth of an heir to the throne, Prince Manuel, son of João III. For the papal nuncio, Aleandro, the play was such a violent satire on Rome and the papacy, that he wrote home that he felt that he was in Saxony hearing a speech from Luther, or in the middle of the horrors of the sack of the Eternal City.[25]

III *The Portuguese-Spanish Production*

The genuine, extant plays by Gil Vicente are forty-four in number. Sixteen of the dramatic pieces are in Portuguese; eleven are in Spanish; and the remaining seventeen combine both languages, with one character speaking one language and another the other. Paul Teyssier has made three good suggestions as to why, at intervals in his career, Gil Vicente wrote in Spanish rather than in his native Portuguese.[26] Literary tradition was a very strong influence upon him in this choice, and, as will be seen almost immediately, he began his dramatic career under the literary influence of the Salamancan dramatists, Juan del Encina and Lucas Fernández. Later on, for example, he wrote two excellent plays of chivalry, based very closely on Spanish novels, and these two plays, as is to be expected from his manner of composing, are in Spanish. In second place, as Teyssier rightly states, is verisimilitude, which causes a Spanish character to be speaking Spanish, while a Portuguese character in the same play will be speaking Portuguese.

And thirdly, it is very true that the Spanish language and culture were held in great esteem and enjoyed great prestige in the Portuguese Court, which was bilingual, in those early years of the sixteenth century. "Successive Kings," wrote Harold V. Livermore, "had put forward dynastic interests in endeavouring to unite the two thrones [of Portugal and Spain] to reign over the whole Peninsula, without apparently much worrying about the consequences to Portugal." [27] Royal marriages between the two countries had indeed been part of monarchical policy from the time of the union of Joana, sister of Portugal's Afonso V, and Enrique IV of Castile, in 1455, up until the noteworthy alliances in Gil Vicente's time: (a) the marriage of Crown Prince Afonso to Princess Isabel, eldest daughter of the Catholic Sovereigns of Spain in 1490 (Prince Afonso was killed in a fall from his horse in 1491, and Isabel went back to Spain); (b) the marriage of Manuel I (1495–1521) to this same Isabel in 1497 (the two were sworn as heirs to Castile and Aragon and went on a grand tour of Spain); (c) the marriage of Manuel I to another daughter of the Catholic Sovereigns, María, in 1500 (their son, João, born in 1502, became João III); (d) the marriage of Manuel I to Leanor, sister of the Emperor Carlos V, in 1518; (e) the marriage of João III (1521–1557) to Catarina, sister of Carlos V, in 1525; and (f) the marriage of João's sister Isabel to Carlos V himself in 1526.

The presence then of so much Spanish influence at the Portuguese Court, in that post-Columbus period when Spain was rising to her height of power in the Western World while Portugal was concerning herself with Africa and the East, and only superficially with Brazil, could not fail to have had its effect on the cultural activities of the Portuguese nation as a whole and on the dramatic poet-at-Court who was concerned with pleasing the Spanish royal ladies and gentlemen, as well as the Portuguese.[28] And while Gil Vicente's writing in both Portuguese and Spanish simultaneously may seem to be an unusual activity, circumstances of the day, when carefully considered, reveal it to be not without logic.

IV *Gil Vicente's Forerunners*

The question arises as to what extent Gil Vicente was the "founder of the Portuguese theater." [29] He was surely the consolidator of what little had gone before him and the innovator of an enriching development. Forerunners of his theatrical art must surely have existed in both Portugal and Spain, for both the religious and the non-religious performances; but almost all examples are non-existent. "When we observe the maturity of certain primitive comic works, like *The Play of India* (*Auto da India*) of Gil Vicente and *The Play of the Legpulling* (*Auto del repelón*) of Encina, both before 1510, we suspect," wrote Eugenio Asensio recently, "that many theatrical seasons have been necessary to bring this maturity about. The leap from juglaresque monologue to dialogue, the conversion of the narrating, gesticulating *juglar* into a dramatic character, seems plain and feasible; but concrete examples to demonstrate the process are lacking." [30]

Documents going back to the twelfth century speak of the existence, in Portugal, of mimicry and imitation (*arremedilhos*), which were farces in embryo; and over the years there were prohibitions recorded against certain abuses in dramatic presentations. In the fifteenth century, to move rapidly forward to pre-Vicentine times, mummeries (*momos*) seem to have been standard court entertainment, and these Gil Vicente must have known intimately and to his profit. A letter of December 25, 1500, from the Spanish ambassador, Ochoa de Ysásaga, to the Catholic Sovereigns, describes at length the Christmas celebrations that year at the Court of Manuel I, and makes specific reference to mummeries. [31]

After religious ceremonies, the letter says, the Court assembled to witness and enjoy the *momos*. The description given of them points forward to Gil Vicente's plays of fantasy, and also to some of his more realistic farces. In the *momos*, various persons wearing masks, to the accompaniment of a musical background, tell stories of "lovers in gardens of love guarded by a dragon." Another person speaks to the Queen and promises her that the King will have victory over his enemies. Another person, humorously and farcically, addresses Her Majesty and asks her to order the ladies not to treat the men so cruelly. As will be seen in later chapters, Gil Vicente did not fail to weave these elements and many others of the kind into his varied repertoire.

For the farce proper, however, there seems to be an immediate forerunner in Anrique da Mota, Gil Vicente's contemporary. Writing in the tradition of the mummeries, he appears in Garcia de

Resende's *Cancioneiro Geral* of 1516, with his *Priest's Lament* (*Pranto do Clérigo*), *The Farce of the Tailor* (*Farsa do Alfaiate*), *The Farce of the Gardener* (*Farsa do Hortelano*), *The Mule's Lament* (*Lamentação da Mula*), and *The Lawsuit of Vasco Abul* (*Processo de Vasco Abul*). To the last named work Gil Vicente contributed some lines of verse, as will be seen in the later study of Miscellaneous Works. The two laments by Anrique da Mota may have inspired Vicente's later *Lament of Maria Parda* (*Pranto de Maria Parda*); and *The Farce of the Tailor* and *The Farce of the Gardener* seem certainly to be the forerunners of several lively Vicentine scenes. In chronology, Anrique da Mota is without doubt the predecessor in *The Farce of the Tailor,* for, as Luciana Stegagno Picchio points out, "The date of death of one of the characters who takes part in the dialogue can be fixed at 1506," [32] a couple of years before Gil Vicente's attention to farce, which began in the period 1508–1509.

Andrée Crabbé Rocha has analysed the portions of the *Cancioneiro Geral* which are of dramatic potentiality.[33] For her, Anrique da Mota is dramatic in a rudimentary way, and the author to be singled out in a search for farcical influences upon Gil Vicente. She stresses the fact that the two "dramatists" have made use more than once of the same comic and burlesque ingredients, such as criticism of the clergy, the presentation of the Jewish convert (the tailor), the ridiculous judge, and the negro or negress speaking a humorous "Portuguese." "Simple grains of sand," concludes the critic, "but they show us however, at least as far as farce is concerned, that Gil Vicente had before him something which resembles a tradition."

If the comic genre offered Gil Vicente fair guidance as he went forward to reach heights of success, the Portuguese religious theater, if it can be said to have existed at all, did not. Surely some rudimentary religious pageants must have been presented from time to time, under Church auspices, but it is the considered conclusion of I. S. Révah, for example, that in writing his "autos de dévotion," Gil Vicente "owed nothing, or almost nothing to a previous Portuguese tradition." [34] In his earlier article on Gil Vicente as the founder of the Portuguese theater, Révah had stressed the same point, asking why Vicente would have imitated the Spanish if the Portuguese theater of the Middle Ages had offered him good examples to follow. But it was the Spanish theater of the Salamancan group that he turned to, in the early years of the fifteen hundreds, to find his guidance. The religious theater was not well developed even in the neighboring country; but Juan del Encina and Lucas Fernández, serving the House of Alba at the end of the fifteenth century, had made a start toward an enrichment which would stand Gil Vicente in good stead. That Spanish *début* will form the substance, as it surely must, of the first chapter on Vicente's dramatic art. Meantime, it is well to conclude this brief account of the life and times of the goldsmith-dramatist by quoting his contemporary at Court, Garcia de Resende:

> And we saw
> Performances, singularly presented,
> In a very eloquent style,
> Filled with many new inventions,
> And prepared by Gil Vicente.
> He was that one who invented
> These things here, and constructed them
> With greater grace and doctrine
> Than ever seen since Juan del Encina
> Began the pastoral style.
>
> (E vimos singularmente
> fazer representações
> de estilo mui eloquente,
> de mui novas invenções,
> e feitas por Gil Vicente.
> Ele foi o que inventou
> isto cá, e o usou
> com mais graça e mais doutrina,
> posto que Juan del Enzina
> o pastoril começou.)

It was this Spaniard Juan del Encina (1469?–1529?), and his contemporary Lucas Fernández (1474?–1542?), both from Salamanca and both palace dramatists of the Duke of Alba, who were Gil Vicente's inspiration and models as he began his dramatic career in 1502, in what may best be called a "Spanish *début*."

CHAPTER 2

The Spanish Début

THE plays which comprise Gil Vicente's *début*, in Spanish, are three: *The Visitation*, or *Herdsman's Monologue* (*Visitação*, or *Monólogo do Vaqueiro*), of June, 1502; *The Castilian Pastoral Play* (*Auto Pastoril Castelhano*), of Christmas, of the same year; and *The Play of the Magi* (*Auto dos Reis Magos*), of Epiphany, 1503. These, as Bell has pointed out, "are especially personal," in that "we may be quite sure that the parts of the herdsman in the *Visitação*, of the mystically inclined shepherd, Gil Terrón, in the *Auto Pastoril Castelhano*, and of the *rústico pastor* in the *Auto dos Reis Magos*, were played by Vicente himself" (*Four Plays*, p. xi).

To these three plays might be added *The Play of St. Martin* (*Auto de S. Martinho*), written for the Corpus Christi celebrations of 1504. The next dramatic efforts, however, are in Portuguese and Spanish, and represent a time-gap of four or five years: *Who Has Bran?* (*Quem Tem Farelos?*) may not have appeared until 1508, *The Play of India* (*Auto da India*), until 1509, and *The Play of Faith* (*Auto da Fé*), until 1510. This unproductive period, in a dramatist who produced quite regularly over his thirty-five years of dramatic activity, may be explained, it is to be remembered, by the fact that Gil Vicente was very busily engaged in his duties as a goldsmith. For example, it is to be recalled that in November, 1503, Vasco da Gama returned to Lisbon from his second voyage to India, and the gold tribute from the East was handed over to Gil Vicente to fashion the famous Belém monstrance, which was completed in 1506.

I The Herdsman's Monologue

In the *Monologue* (text to be found in the *Obras completas*, I, 1–7), the herdsman enters Queen Maria's bedchamber to congratulate her, and King Manuel, on the birth of their first-born son

(João III). He relates, in verse of eight, and occasionally four, syllables, that the palace servants have tried to prevent his coming in. Amid his wonder at the splendor of the royal apartment, he goes on to explain that he has been sent by his village to ascertain whether the glorious event has really taken place. He then praises the royal parents and grandparents, and predicts that the royal child will be as great as his ancestors. Finally, Gil Vicente, in the person of the herdsman, reveals that he has thirty comrades outside who have gifts of eggs, milk, cheese and honey, and he calls them in to present their gifts.

The language used in this short dramatic monologue, of some 112 lines, is rustic Spanish, the dialectal *sayagués,* in imitation of the Salamancan Juan del Encina.[1] Gil Vicente, on this occasion and on many others, showed great sensitivity to the comic potentialities inherent in popular speech. His choice of Spanish was due, first of all, to his desire to use the language most pleasing to the young Spanish-speaking queen away from home, and at the same time most pleasing and acceptable to the many courtiers and ladies-in-waiting of the Spanish retinue. But literary tradition, however, was no doubt a powerful influence upon this first dramatic essay too, for as Joseph A. Meredith put it in his study of the sixteenth-century *introito* and *loa,* "Encina's usage determined the form of the *Visitação,* or *Monólogo do Vaqueiro,* in which with pastoral garb and language, Gil Vicente offered congratulations to King Manuel and Queen Maria of Portugal on the birth of Prince John."[2]

One may immediately ask how Gil Vicente, living in Portugal, knew the works of the Salamancan dramatist; but it has been stated on many occasions, very properly, that Juan del Encina's *Cancionero* of 1496 early reached the library of the Portuguese Court. It is even possible that Gil Vicente may have witnessed the performance of some of Encina's eclogues in the higher circles of his native land; and there can be no doubt but that he had Juan del Encina's works in mind—and those of Lucas Fernández too, also early available to him—when in later years in a prologue to the *Copilação,* directed to João III, he spoke of "The books which I saw written . . ." ("Os livros das obras que escritas vi . . .") (*Obras completas,* I, lxxix). The literary idea for the *Monólogo do Vaqueiro* seems to have been directly inspired by the preliminary words to Encina's first *Eclogue,* in which the shepherd Juan enters the palace hall, where the Duke and Duchess of Alba have been hearing matins, to address an appreciative monologue to the Duchess before turning to praise the Duke. In both cases, we have a *pièce de circonstance,* an "occasion play," and we are on the borderline between the recitation of literary material and the dramatization of such material. "The play resembles the first and fifth eclogues of Encina," wrote Ronald B. Williams, "in that it consists of real events pictured as they happen, with individuals in the audience addressed directly, and it resembles all of the first eight Encina pieces in that it treats only one theme and confines the action to a single place." [3]

II   The Castilian Pastoral Play

The Castilian Pastoral Play (*Obras completas,* I, 9–31), which was written at the request of the dowager Queen Leanor for the Christmas court festivities of 1502, is a "pastoral colloquium in the Juan del Encina manner" ("un coloquio pastoril a lo Juan del Encina"), to use the words of Bruce W. Wardropper.[4] A shepherd Gil, full of simple, deep faith, does not enter into the usual pastoral frivolities, and is able to hear the song of the angels proclaiming the birth of the Christ Child. He then persuades his less spiritual companions to go with him to adore Jesus, and they all present gifts amid much singing, dancing, and rejoicing.

Here we have a development of, and an improvement upon, the previous means of explaining Christ's birth: Juan del Encina made indirect use of an angel in his second eclogue; Lucas Fernández made use of a hermit in his *Eclogue or Farce on the Birth of Our Redeemer Jesus Christ* (*Egloga o Farsa del Nacimiento de Nuestro Redemptor Jesucristo*); and Gil Vicente's agent is his contemplative shepherd. This Gil Terrón stands apart from his fellows, as has been noted. By the grace of God perhaps—concerning his unusual knowledge he says near the end of the play that "God performs these miracles" ("Dios hace estas maravillas") —he knows all of the prophecies concerning the miraculous birth, and, in addition, even the Latin language! Juan del Encina's first two eclogues apparently inspired Lucas Fernández's *Egloga o Farsa del Nacimiento,* written about 1500, and all three works of the Salamancan dramatists were probably before Vicente as he prepared his *Auto Pastoril Castelhano*. The influences from Encina are at best vague; but a specific influence from Lucas Fernández, as John Lihani has stated, is "the genealogical recitations of the shepherds in the plays of the respective writers." [5] Both Lihani and Teyssier, in his monograph on Gil Vicente's language, point particularly to the declaration of good lineage made by Bras-Gil in Lucas Fernández's first comedy (ca. 1496), the *Comedy of Bras-Gil and Beringuella* (*Comedia de Bras-Gil y Beringuella*), which was apparently closely followed by Vicente when he had his shepherd Gil recite the family background of the wife of his friend Silvestre.

III   The Portuguese Pastoral Play

It is worth while noting at this point that Gil Vicente wrote a companion-piece, *The Portuguese Pastoral Play* (*Auto Pastoril Português*) many years later, in 1523 (text in *Obras completas*, I, 163–194). This is a Christmas play, written for the Court in residence at Evora. The play begins with a comical prologue recited by a peasant from Beira, and in the prologue the audience is told that shepherds and shepherdesses, from the Serra da Estrêla, will, amid singing and dancing, discuss and worry about their love affairs. Friars will appear too, the peasant relates, friars "who have just been stealing melons." Amid general merrymaking, singing, dancing, and guessing games, one shepherdess reveals that she has found an image of the Virgin Mary. Four priests intone a beautiful hymn of praise in sonorous twelve-syllable lines, and the play ends gaily in dancing, and in the singing by all of a sprightly song: "Who is the bride? / The Holy Virgin. . . ." ("Quem é a desposada? / A Virgem sagrada. . . .")

The above-mentioned prologue is a type of introduction which was used frequently by the Spanish Torres Naharro in his plays (his collection of works, the *Propaladia*, was published in 1517), and it is likely that Gil Vicente once more was making use of the Spanish theater to enrich his dramatic offerings. It is most interesting, likewise, in Gil Vicente's prologue that the shepherd has met "a Gil who prepares plays for the King" ("um Gil . . . que faz os autos a elrei") and who has not a penny. Related to this last detail are contemporary accounts which declare that the dramatist did receive a gift of coins from the King in May, 1523, and that in

1524, he was in receipt of a small pension. Perhaps the very pointed words had their effect! But the whole tone, throughout the little work, is jocular (with due respect apparent in the praise of the Virgin); and the play is one more "occasion piece," to entertain, and incidentally, to edify, the Portuguese Court.

IV   The Play of the Magi

But back to the Spanish *début! The Play of the Magi* (text in *Obras completas*, I, 33–47) presented at Epiphany, 1503, provides even greater variety than before, and greater development, through the addition of both a knight and a hermit. Again following in the style and manner of Juan del Encina and of Lucas Fernández, Gil Vicente presents to his audience the shepherd Gregorio, who has heard the voice of an angel tell him to leave his flocks and go seek the Child Jesus. As he and a companion wander about, they fall in with a hermit (treated comically and satirically) and a knight who has come from Arabia to join the three Wise Men, who are on their way, the audience is told, to pay homage to the new-born Savior. The Wise Kings are not the main characters of the play, in spite of the title, but at the very end they do appear on stage, to sing the beautiful Christmas carol (*vilancete*): "When the blessèd Virgin / Gave birth to the Savior. . . ." ("Cuando la Virgen bendita / lo parió. . . ."). Apparently a crèche was a part of the simple setting, for at the final moment, the Magi offer their presents, and leave the stage singing joyfully.

This going-to-Bethlehem to adore the new-born Christ-child is found at the end of both of Lucas Fernández's Christmas farces (*farsas del nacimiento*), and this way of ending the *Auto dos Reis Magos* may have come from him. Furthermore, Fray Ambrosio Montesino's *Epistles and Evangels for the Whole Year* (*Epístolas y evangelios para todo el año*) and Ludolphus de Saxonia's *Life of Christ* (*Vita Christi*), in translation, were popular reading in Portugal at that time, and these pious works could have supplied details for the Portuguese Court dramatist, as Thomas R. Hart has pointed out in his edition of the *Auto dos Reis Magos*.[6] The knight's description of a star with the figure of a child in the middle of it is found in both of these works. Also, another *Life of Christ*, the *Vita Christi* by Fray Iñigo de Mendoza, turned into Spanish for the edification of the faithful unfamiliar with Latin, was owned by the dowager Queen Leanor, and was very well known to Gil Vicente. This last was a long didactic poem containing a Nativity play, which in itself must not have failed to influence the Portuguese dramatist.[7]

V The Play of St. Martin

Of the eighty-line *Play of St. Martin* (*Obras completas*, II, 265–269), it is sufficient to say that although it has been called the first *auto sacramental*, the play does not belong to that *genre*. It is a simple, poetic presentation of the well-known episode of St. Martin's sharing his cloak with the beggar, and of slight literary significance. In the play, which was performed in the Caldas Church, during the Corpus Christi celebrations of 1504, the wealthy Martin, accompanied by three pages, heeds the poor man's plea, and with his sword divides his garment in two. Laurence Keates was right when he wrote that "Vicente's play is short and wooden in its versification. He realized instinctively that the life of a saint, being perfectly predictable after a radical conversion or the attainment of a certain stage of perfection (when the will of the saint becomes fused with God's will for him) is not fit material for drama, which relies for its effectiveness on the continuing possibility of choice between good and evil." [8]

St. Martin has received considerable attention from the compilers of anthologies of the Spanish religious theater during the last one hundred years, because in literary history it is a forerunner of later and better works of the kind.[9] But as far as Gil Vicente's dramatic production is concerned, it belongs to the Spanish *début* only because of its date, and language-connection with the other earliest works.

William C. Atkinson has severely criticized Gil Vicente's "failure" to learn dramatic technique for use in later plays as being "almost incredible in a follower of Encina";[10] but I. S. Révah declares, more correctly, that "Gil Vicente has followed brilliantly in the footsteps of Juan del Encina and of Lucas Fernández in the *Auto Pastoril Castelhano* . . . , and indirectly in the *Auto dos Reis Magos*." [11] As Révah also says, Juan del Encina, in his second eclogue, "had started the tradition," and had, as Joseph A. Meredith put it, "set a precedent which was to have a direct effect on the development of the early drama as a whole." Bruce W. Wardropper, in studying the Vicentine chivalric tragicomedies in 1964, credits Juan del Encina with the "secularizaton of the *Officium Pastorum* tradition," and credits Gil Vicente with going far beyond Juan del Encina, in later plays, "into complex secular dramas." [12] "If Encina," wrote Wardropper, "treading carefully and surely, followed a straight line from liturgical play to amorous tragicomedy, Gil Vicente might be said to have scurried in all possible directions. In his complete works one perceives no straight line, no sure goal, no clear purpose, no inevitable tendency. He explores all the avenues leading to and from the great square of the *Officium Pastorum*."

In the case of *The Play of Faith* (*Auto da Fé*), of 1510, for example, Révah points out that Gil Vicente "was still searching at that date how to bring about the renewing of the Salamancan formula of the Christmas play." And Eugenio Asensio, in discussing the later *Play of the Four Seasons* (*Auto dos Quatro Tempos*), of 1516?, believes Gil Vicente to have been a success, rather than a failure as Atkinson would have it, as a follower of the Salamancan dramatists. "He began by going to the school of Encina and Lucas Fernández," wrote Asensio. "Soon he surpassed the primitive formulae of the Salamancans and attempted to renew the presentation of the eternal themes of the Encarnation and Redemption. He opened new paths, he widened the old ones. . . ." [13]

The Spanish *début*, it might be said in concluding this chapter, was a brief period of pastoral experimentation. It was a fleeting moment in Vicente's long dramatic career, and not of high literary significance in itself, if we evaluate the total Vicentine picture. Nevertheless, the Spanish *début* was a time for exploration, a time for building upon and testing certain elements of the past. After this dramatic apprenticeship, and some years devoted to the goldsmith's trade, Gil Vicente was prepared and ready to continue with what Asensio has called "new poetic adventures."

CHAPTER 3

The Continuation of the Salamancan Tradition

AS has been said in the preceding chapter, Gil Vicente made good use of his Spanish *début* to evolve into an enriched and more significant later dramatic postion. In his exploration of "all the avenues leading to and from the great square of the *Officium Pastorum*," he did not forget or cast aside the Salamancan influence which had profited him to such a great extent. At the time when he conceived his *Play of Faith* (*Auto da Fé*), of 1510, after the period devoted to the goldsmith's trade and to experimentation with farce, with *Who Has Bran?* (*Quem Tem Farelos?*), of 1508?, and *The Play of India* (*Auto da India*), of 1509?, he was still involved in meditating upon the continuation and development of the Salamancan Christmas play. And his interest did not quickly die, for the later *Play of the Sibyl Cassandra* (*Auto da Sibila Cassandra*), of 1513 or 1514, and *The Play of the Four Seasons* (*Auto dos Quatro Tempos*), of 1516,—and even his second-last piece, *The Play of Mofina Mendes* (*Auto da Mofina Mendes*) of 1534—have a continuing relationship with the Spanish *début* as represented by the *Visitação*, the *Auto Pastoril Castelhano*, and the *Auto dos Reis Magos*.

I The Play of Faith

The Play of Faith (text in *Obras completas*, I, 83–96), in Portuguese and in Spanish, of some 330 lines, is definitely a continuation of the Spanish pastoral style of Juan del Encina and Lucas Fernández . This slight play, presented on Christmas Day, 1510, after matins, before King Manuel and his Court assembled at Almeirim, is simply a conversation between the allegorical figure Faith and two peasants. Faith, speaking Portuguese, explains to the peasants, who speak Encina-like Spanish, the meaning of the marvels which they see in the chapel at Christmas time. The laden table, the holy water, the tree of life, the crown of thorns, the cross—all evoke many questions and the corresponding pious answers; but above all, details of Christ's birth are the center of discussion: born of the Blessed Virgin, in a humble manner, 1510 years before. . . . In the dénouement, the two shepherds call a third, and they celebrate the joyful event, singing with Faith, a song "which came from France" (not given).

II The Play of the Sibyl Cassandra

If the *Auto da Fé* is a play simple and unpretentious to the extreme, the next play by Gil Vicente in this Salamancan tradition, *The Play of the Sibyl Cassandra* (of 1513 or 1514) is complicated and highly developed. (The text is to be found in *Obras completas*, I, 49–82.) This longer play, of about 800 lines, in Spanish, was probably performed before Queen Leanor, after Christmas matins, in the Convent of Enxobregas, Lisbon. There are many reminiscences in it of Juan del Encina and of Lucas Fernández, but the treatment of the old Christmas story is new and complex, far from the primitive simplicity of the dramatists of Salamanca.

The plot of the *Auto da Sibila Cassandra* is, in brief, a discussion of the shepherdess Cassandra's refusal to marry, because, for her, matrimony is a kind of slavery. And, in addition, later in the play, she reveals another bold thought which is in her mind: that she will be the virgin chosen by God to be the mother of the Redeemer! Therefore she rejects the handsome young shepherd, Solomon, who in due time seeks the aid, to no avail, of her aunts, the sibyls Erutea, Peresica, and Cimeria. Solomon also appeals to his uncles, the prophets Moses, Abraham, and Isaiah. But no one can overcome Cassandra's obstinacy, and when she finally reveals that she must preserve her virginity since the Son of God will be born of a virgin, all are aghast at her temerity and presumption. For the sibyls and prophets in the play, Christ will be born of a selfless virgin chosen for her humility; and in the presentation of the Christmas theme, each has a comment to make on coming events. Erutea prophesies that the new-born child will be born in a manger and will be visited by both shepherds and kings; Cimeria presents a vision of the Virgin and her Son, who will have a great following; Peresica foretells the Crucifixion; and other prophecies are uttered, including that of the Last Judgment.

At this point, a curtain is drawn aside dramatically, and the manger is seen. The characters of the play approach amid dancing and merry-making to worship the new-born Savior and to glorify His Mother. Only Cassandra is bashfully hesitant, asking the Virgin to intercede for her with her Son and begging pardon for such a presumptuous error. The play ends amid continuing dancing and with two delightful songs: "How comely the Maiden, / How lovely and fair" and "Go forth to war, / Ye gallant knights," both of which merit further comment below.

The *Auto da Sibila Cassandra* has proven to be of sufficient dramatic value and interest to have attracted the attention of several important modern critics. Georgiana Goddard King, a professor of the History of Art at Bryn Mawr College and a member of the Hispanic Society of America, in 1921 dedicated a short monograph to a discussion of the value of the play.[1] In the same year an excellent edition of the play appeared in Madrid by one "Alvaro Giráldez," who in reality was the well-known *vicentista*, Aubrey Fitz Gerald Bell. Very recently, Thomas R. Hart has devoted a penetrating article to it,[2] as have María Rosa Lida de Malkiel,[3] Leo Spitzer,[4] and I. S. Révah.[5] In addition, Thomas R. Hart has presented us with the text, plus an introduction and notes, in his above-mentioned *Obras dramáticas castellanas*.

It is pointed out by the critics, and especially by María Rosa Lida de Malkiel, that the main source of the play is an Italian novel of chivalry, Andrea da Barberino's *Guerino meschino*, which had been translated into Spanish by Alonso Hernández Alemán, and published in Seville by Jacobo Cromberger in 1512. In the Italian novel, Guerino, who is seeking his lost parents, is sent to a sibyl, Cumana, who has been intent on preserving her virginity because she believes that God incarnate will be born of her. There is also mention of other sibyls found in the Vicente play: Erutea, and a Cassandra, and in addition a Sabá of Arabia (Queen of Sheba), whose name immediately suggests Solomon, with whom she is associated. The name Cassandra, María Rosa de Lida Malkiel points out, was a name old in literature and a name very well known to Gil Vicente. The sibyl Cassandra was a daughter of King Priam of Troy, and Gil Vicente had been referring recently to the *Crónica Troyana* in the preparation of his *Exhortation to War* (*Exhortação da Guerra*), of 1513.

Georgiana Goddard King, the art historian, it is to be recalled, pointed out that Church iconography frequently portrayed Solomon and a sibyl; perhaps Solomon and the Queen of Sheba, or Solomon and Cassandra, who had become in medieval literature through variation in names the prophetess of Christ's coming. I. S. Révah, in his article on the play, mentioned that the church door of the monastery of Tomar portrays, among other figures, a bearded man and a woman in ecstatic adoration. These Révah believes to be a sibyl and Solomon. Gil Vicente, the goldsmith, we remember, was overseer of the artifacts in gold and silver at the Monastery of Tomar from 1509 to 1513. The Tomar doorway is dated "1515." It is very possible that the figures portrayed on this church door have an iconographic connection with Vicente's dramatic version of the story of the sibyl Cassandra.

The interpretation given to *The Play of the Sibyl Cassandra* by Thomas R. Hart in both his article in *Hispanic Review* and in the introduction to his edition is an allegorical one; and Hart insists that Gil Vicente is deeply involved in an intention of "saying one thing to mean another." The critic enters into a very careful and detailed analysis of the play to move from what he calls the *sensus* (the first, apparent meaning) to the *sententia* (the allegorical meaning); the second, Hart insists, being much more important. On the other hand, it must be interjected, María Rosa Lida de Malkiel, in her study of the play, rejects the allegorical interpretation, chiefly on the grounds that pious works like this one would have little effect if put in terms which had to be deciphered.

Cassandra's opening declaration that she is unwilling to enter into the slavery of marriage is interpreted by Hart to refer to "the spiritual marriage of the Christian soul and Christ." But María Rosa objects to this interpretation on the grounds that it is difficult to then bring in the fact that Cassandra is wanting to be the mother of Christ. Solomon, Hart insists, is a *figura Christi*, "so that Cassandra in refusing to marry Solomon is rejecting the spiritual marriage with Christ as well." Solomon owns orchards and vineyards; and the apple and wine, being symbols of Christ, are put forth by Hart to strengthen his interpretation of Solomon's real significance. Strangely enough, however, Solomon owns thirty-two hens, and the number thirty-two is puzzling. The hen may symbolize Christ, through Jesus' words in Matthew XXIII, 37: "Jerusalem, Jerusalem, thou that killest the prophets, and stonest them that are sent unto thee, how often would I have gathered together thy children, as the hen doth gather her chickens under her wings, and thou wouldest not?" But the number thirty-two is puzzling to Hart, for thirty-three, the number of years which Jesus spent on earth, would fit the symbolism better. And Hart can only conclude hesitantly that "perhaps the number thirty-two refers to the completed year of Christ's life on earth." "Allegorically," concludes Hart, "thirty-two would be highly appropriate, since it is a multiple of four, which symbolizes the world, and eight, the number of resurrection and hence of Christ."

Thomas R. Hart continues deeply in his allegorical interpretation to discuss adjectives which refer to Cassandra and the others; to discuss the symbolism of the gifts offered to Cassandra by Abraham, Moses, and Isaiah, and Solomon himself; and to discuss the juxtaposition, within the play, of the Last Judgment and the birth of the Messiah. But Leo Spitzer, in his rejoinder to Hart, in the above-mentioned article in *Hispanic Review*, 1959, urges a more literal interpretation of the play; and one which is surely closer to Gil Vicente's intention. There is a great danger in reading into literary works meaning which the author may certainly never have thought of, and unless clear clues and indications are put forth by the author himself or by reliable contemporaries— and we have none of these in the case of the *Sibyl Cassandra*—we must be very wary of misinterpretation.

I. S. Révah, in his article on the play, dismisses Hart's theories in an almost sarcastic way: "We shall present only one objection to Hart's subtle interpretation: if Gil Vicente had wished to speak of the spiritual marriage of the Christian soul and Christ to his spectators, without doubt he would have taken the trouble to warn them of his intention." María Rosa Lida de Malkiel, it is to be recalled, put forth the same idea, making a general comment of great validity: "Allegory as a method of literary interpretation is a natural product of the irrationalism and anti-historicism dear to our century, it escapes all objective verification, and has no other law nor guide than the skill of the interpreter to 'discover' in the text all that he in fact wishes to find. . . ." The play, insists

María Rosa, gives no indication of any necessary decipherment. She admits that Cassandra may vaguely symbolize humanity, and that Mary glorified, which is the climax of the play, may be humility glorified; but she states that the play does not need an allegorical key to reveal its unity and significance, and that "the allegorization of detail" (thirty-two hens, etc.) must be completely rejected. These, if valid, would in María Rosa's opinion, be comprehensible only to one familiar with Scripturists of the eleventh and twelfth centuries, and Gil Vicente possessed too great a dramatic instinct to direct himself to a theological audience in a work directed to the Court. But, concludes María Rosa Lida de Malkiel, is it not useless to require logic in a method set up expressly to elude it? And to drive home her valid point, she refers us to a statement by Helen Gardner: "I cannot feel satisfied with a literary criticism which substitutes for the conception of the writer as 'a man speaking to men,' the conception of the writer as an imagination weaving symbolic patterns to be teased out by the intellect, and in the concentration on the work by itself ends by finding significance in what the work suggests rather than in what it says. . . . It is the first responsibility of an interpreter that he should neither disregard nor damage that first freshness with which things made by long-dead men speak directly to the mind and heart." [6]

In this knotty problem of the meaning of Gil Vicente's *Auto da Sibila Cassandra,* it is well to give most careful attention to Spitzer's careful analysis, in addition to Hart's, for Spitzer singles out many of the latter's statements and makes intelligent comments on them. Spitzer, first of all, praises the Hart study for its painstaking analysis, and for its proof "that the play has inner unity and coherence." However, Spitzer hastens to point out that other readers may see "the undoubtable unity of the *auto* in a different light." The "different light" in Spitzer's case, then, is the above-mentioned more literal interpretation, to modify drastically Hart's out and out allegorical interpretation. Spitzer is willing to pick up some of Hart's phrases, and add some of his own, as worthy of a deeper than literal meaning. Spitzer, for example, makes a good point in singling out Cassandra's use of the word "birth" near the beginning of the play, where she declares that her attitude toward marriage was born when she was born. "With this remark," writes Spitzer, "there is mentioned for the first time the theme of 'birth' which will be so important throughout this Nativity play: we must anticipate at this point that the loveless Cassandra will need to be re-born—into love." In Cassandra's reference to herself as a flower, Spitzer follows Hart's reference to the Virgin Mary, "the perfect flower, rose, or lily." But in many, many lines which Hart considers to be allegorical, Spitzer finds only "pure badinage without any mystic overtones." These comic features are very frequent, for after all the audience wanted to be entertained, and as will be pointed out in a later chapter, Gil Vicente was a master of farce; and especially in the early part of this play that mastery in farce is clearly perceived. The early Cassandra is a comical figure in her disdain for marriage, as is Solomon, "this carefree, narcissistic shepherd . . . a quite worldly lover, unsophisticatedly selfsatisfied with his family background [the previously mentioned shepherd's pride in lineage], his manners and his economic position"—a naïvely rude young man, "taking it for granted that the maiden will and must marry him."

In fact, Spitzer feels that in this low-level, earthy opening of the play, we are on the level of the word-battles between Petruchio and Katherine in *The Taming of the Shrew*. Solomon is not yet the wise Solomon, the King of the Old Testament, but he will assume that lofty position at the end of the play. Cassandra too will undergo a sudden change as she begs forgiveness for her criminal intent, and takes her place "in the group of those who worship the coming of the Savior." But in the early scenes farce is uppermost, and the tone of the play is jocular at this time when Solomon is pressing his suit and boasting of his worldly wealth, including the thirty-two hens! These thirty-two hens which Hart took such great pains to explain allegorically have, in Spitzer's ear (which, he confesses "is not an allegorical one"), "a distinctly jocular ring." "Solomon is here," adds Spitzer, "not yet an almighty King, but a small chicken farmer, proud of what he owns."

Spitzer meditates upon the reason for Solomon's double rôle. His decision is that "Gil Vicente obviously composed his play not according to the requirements of psychological consistency, but as has been shown (by Levin Schücking) for some of Shakespeare's plays, according to the logic of the different particular scenes."

This same "scene-wise composition" is found also in the presentation of the sibyls. In their first appearance, they are really only "good-hearted" aunts trying to arrange their niece's marriage, in the absence of a deceased mother. Their later, and historic, rôle as prophetesses comes farther on in the play. For the rôle of prophecy they do assume, as has been seen, to make prophecy, in Spitzer's opinion, "the play's central theme." Spitzer makes a very good point when he declares that "*All* the dramatis personae assume the rôle of 'prophets' and all, except Cassandra, are prophets of Christ's birth from Mary: the Old Testamentary patriarchs Abraham, Moses and Isaiah (and also Solomon) as well as the Sibyls." In this compressing of history and the abandonment of chronological time, "we have before us the well-known topos of prefiguration or *Realprophetie* as the late Professor Auerbach has called the figurative-anticipative linking, in patristic and vernacular medieval literature, of pre-Christian figures and events with Christian figures and events in which they culminate. . . ."

J. P. Wickersham Crawford feels that it is the "lovely lyrics" of the play "that constitute its chief charm." [7] Indeed, Aubrey Fitz Gerald Bell declares that "In the *Auto da Sibila Cassandra* Vicente appears for the first time as a marvelous lyric poet" (*Lyrics*, p. viii). Cecil M. Bowra finds that Vicente "uses the resources of tradition for a poetry which is always fresh and graceful and gay";[8] and Dámaso Alonso finds five delightful songs in this play.[9] The first song is sung by Cassandra herself, as she rejects Solomon's suit: "They would have me wed, but I / Truly for no husband sigh" ("Dicen que me case yo; / No quiero marido, no"). —Alonso, No. 4, p. 25; Bell, No. 51, pp. 108–109. The popularity and literary value of this first song have been proven by the fact that George Ticknor translated it over a hundred years ago ("They say, ' 'Tis time, go marry go!' But I'll no husband! Not I! no!"),[10] and the song itself was chosen by James Fitzmaurice-Kelly for *The Oxford Book of Spanish Verse*.

The second *cantiga* (Dámaso Alonso's No. 5, p. 26: "¡Qué sañosa está la niña! / ¡Ay Dios! ¿quién le hablaría?") is the delightful composition which is sung by Solomon, Isaiah, Moses, and Abraham, as they comment on Cassandra's resistance to love. The Ticknor translation (*History*, p. 287) reads as follows:

She is wild! She is wild!
Who shall speak to the child?
On the hills pass her hours,
As a shepherdess free;
She is fair as the flowers,
She is wild as the sea!
She is wild! She is wild!
Who shall speak to the child?

("¡Qué sañosa está la niña! / ¡Ay Dios! ¿quién le hablaría? / En la sierra anda la niña / su ganado a repastar; / hermosa como las flores, / sañosa como la mar. / Sañosa como la mar / está la niña. / ¡Ay Dios! ¿quién le hablaría?")

Later, toward the end of the play, as the curtains are drawn back to reveal the Nativity scene,[11] four angels sing to the Child Jesus a beautiful lullaby: "Sleep Thou, O sleep, / Our God and our Redeemer, / Since grief when Thou dost weep / Thou givest Thy Virgin Mother . . ." ("Ro ro ro / nuestro Dios y Redentor, / no lloréis, que dais dolor / a la virgen que os parió. / Ro ro ro.") —Alonso, No. 6, p. 27; Bell, No. 30, pp. 62–63. Bell, in his note to the song, prints a Latin fragment which is very similar and which may have inspired Gil Vicente on this occasion:

Dormi, Jesu, mater ridet
Quae tam dulcem somnum videt,
Dormi, Jesu blandule,
Si non dormis mater plorat,
Inter fila cantans orat:
Blande veni somnule.

At the end of the play, those assembled on the stage sing in praise of the Blessed Virgin, as they dance three by three, a song which Dámaso Alonso says was composed by Gil Vicente himself, indeed one of the few we know he wrote, for he often made use of songs then extant. Ticknor's version (*History*, p. 288) runs thus: "The maid is gracious and fair; / How beautiful beyond compare"; and Bell renders it in this way "How comely the Maiden, / How lovely and fair" (Bell, No. 34, pp. 70–71). The Spanish text ("Muy graciosa es la doncella; / ¡cómo es bella y hermosa!") is Alonso's No. 7, p. 28, and was also included in Fitzmaurice-Kelly's *Oxford*

Book of Spanish Verse. Bell's note also states that this lyric "has been compared (as to the metre) with Robert Browning's 'Nay, but you who do not love her, / Is she not pure gold, my mistress?'" "But Browning," continues Bell, "had not the lyrical genius of Vicente, which gleams here like the evening star when shepherds fold their flocks or waters stilled at even."

This lyric, as Spitzer reminds us in his article, forms part of the final scenes of the play "toward which the previous scenes had been pointing with ever growing dramatic intensity." It is a great operatic scene, claims Spitzer, "a *Gesamtkunstwerk* appealing to the different senses in which poetry, music (the singing first of the angels, then of the patriarchs), the plastic arts (the *tableau vivant* of Mary feeding the child in the manger, both remaining silent) and dance (the final *terreiro*) participate in order to celebrate the joy of a world to whom the Savior has come, the joyful harmony that can fitly be represented only in a display of all the arts in which musical harmony takes the lead." "It is," says Spitzer, "as if the whole final scene of the Adoration were staged for [Cassandra] especially, for her conversion, for her entrance into the fold of the believers." The harmony which had been disturbed by Cassandra alone, through her personal hybris and her consequent tragic isolation, is now reestablished as she bows before the Mother of God and her Holy Son.

Attached to the play, at the very end, is an "exhortation to war," a spirited call to arms, which, according to Dámaso Alonso, has no connection with the play proper: "Go forth to war, / Ye gallant knights, / Since the angels from heights / Come to help us upon earth. / Go forth!" ("A la guerra, / Caballeros esforzados: / pues los ángeles sagrados / a socorro son en tierra. / ¡A la guerra!")— Alonso, No. 8, p. 29; Bell, No. 43, pp. 92–93. Thomas R. Hart, however, considers the song to be an integral part of the *Sibyl Cassandra*, and he finds for it an allegorical meaning, as he continues his allegorical analysis. For him, the gallant knights must be understood as referring to all Christians, "for every Christian is, figuratively at least, a *miles Christi*, a soldier for Christ." "This is, I think," continues Hart, "the *raison d'être* of the military imagery which occurs here and there throughout the play and on which we have already had occasion to comment. It is significant that Cassandra herself joins in the singing of the final song, for the song, far from being unrelated to the rest of the play, is at once Cassandra's acceptance of the rôle she must play in the world and an appeal to every member of the audience to accept a similar double rôle as *sponsa* and *miles Christi.*"

Aubrey F. G. Bell (under the pseudonym of Alvaro Giráldez), however, in his Madrid, 1921, edition of the play, had expressed the commonly held opinion of the exhortation's place and purpose: "This final song has nothing to do with the subject of the *auto;* it refers doubtless to one of the frequent wars in which the Portuguese were engaged in Africa." Spitzer in his article on *The Sibyl Cassandra* supports this position: "Siding with Menéndez Pelayo and other critics, I consider our song ('How comely the maiden, / How lovely and fair') as the true end of the play in which all the actors on stage (including the author) dance a final round, and the 'fare-well *villancico*' 'A la guerra, caballeros esforzados' as a *poésie de circonstance* reflecting contemporary patriotic sentiment . . . , comparable to the playing of the national anthem at the end of a dramatic performance in war time." To those who have lived through the twentieth century's many turbulent years, when a national anthem has indeed been played and played at the beginning or at the end of public functions, Spitzer's idea is very logical and acceptable. The Portuguese were deeply involved in their religious battles in North Africa (in those years when they were also involved in expansion in the East), and "To war, gallant knights" had a very real meaning in a *literal* and practical application to the times.

"So, when in the *Auto da Sibila Cassandra*," writes Bowra, "[Gil Vicente] decided to write a song for one of the periodical Portuguese expeditions to Africa, he had not only to find a form for a subject which was hardly treated at all by popular song, but to accommodate his matter to the current notion that such expeditions were crusades in which God and His Saints fought on the side of the Christians against the infidels. The result is a stirring little piece 'fit for the gaiety of Mozart,' a *vilancete* in traditional form adapted to the high crisis." Very clear it is then that the Hart explanation and interpretation is to be rejected, and the real function and purpose of the song, as a disconnected exhortation to patriotism, is to be reestablished within the framework of the Vicentine dramatic art.

III   The Exhortation to War

This stirring call to action, attached artificially to the *Sibyl Cassandra,* reminds us that Gil Vicente did write a complete play, in Portuguese, entitled *The Exhortation to War* (*Exhortação da Guerra*) at about the same time as *The Play of the Sibyl Cassandra.* (The text of *Exhortação da Guerra* is to be found in *Obras completas,* IV, 127–157, and also, with English translation, in Bell's *Four Plays of Gil Vicente,* pp. 23–35). This *Exhortation to War,* says Bell (*Four Plays,* p. 75), "was the first of the great patriotic outbursts . . . in which Vicente appears not as a satirist or religious reformer but as an enthusiastic imperialist, and which still delight and stir his countrymen."

The rubric in the 1562 *Copilação* states that the play was given before King Manuel in Lisbon on the occasion of the departure for Azamor, North West Africa, of an expedition under James, Duke of Braganza, in August, 1513. This date is accepted by Bell, but António José Saraiva[12] dates the play as "1514" through internal allusions to the King's obtaining, in 1514, permission from Rome to preempt one third of ecclesiastical revenues to aid in the African war, and to Tristão da Cunha's mission to the Holy See, in the same year, when an elephant was presented to the Pope. (Bell explains the presence of these allusions in the play by stating that the play was probably touched up after 1513.) These problems of dating are very difficult indeed, and since the rubrics of the *Copilação* are sometimes inaccurate, it will be close enough to decide upon 1513–1514 for this dramatic piece.

IV   The Play of Fame

In this theatrical exhortation, in which Gil Vicente comes forth "as the poet laureate of the nation," vehemently inveighing "against sloth and luxury while he sings a hymn to the glories of Portugal" (Bell, *Four Plays,* p. 44), the great men of the past—Achilles, Hannibal, Hector, and Scipio—urge the Portuguese forward to continue their glorious mission, while Hannibal sings "On, on! Go forward, lord and knight, / Since in war waged for the right / God as captain leads the fight" ("Avante! avante! Senhores! / que na guerra com razão / anda Deus por capitão"). The same inspirational tone is put forth too in *The Play of Fame*

(*Auto da Fama*), in Portuguese and Spanish (the text is to be found in *Obras completas,* V, 117–140). This drama, which may belong to the year 1515, allegorizes the glories of Portuguese maritime discoveries and military achievements: the siege of Goa (1510), the capture of Malaca (1511), the victorious expedition against Azamor (1513), and the attack on Aden (1513). Portuguese fame is being much envied and sought after by all nations, as the preliminary résumé in the *Copilação* says, not only because of her growing world commerce, but especially since Portugal is winning so many victories over the Mohammedans, the enemies of the Faith. Specifically in the play, Fame is courted by a Frenchman (speaking a kind of French), by an Italian (speaking a kind of Italian), and by a Castilian (naturally speaking Spanish). She rejects them all to remain in Portugal; and at the end of this Court allegory of a patriotic nature, Fame is crowned with a laurel wreath by Faith and Fortitude, and is carried off the stage in a triumphal car amid much general rejoicing.

Neither *The Exhortation to War* nor *The Play of Fame* belongs to the continuation of the Salamancan tradition, but it seemed à propos to include them in this chapter through their connection with the "unconnected" final patriotic song to be found at the end of *The Play of the Sibyl Cassandra,* which must still hold our attention as we devote to it some final words before going on to others of the "Salamancan" grouping. Away back in the mid-nineteenth century George Ticknor (*History,* pp. 288–289) had commented at length on the play; and while he did not completely approve of it nor understand it his words gave food for thought and discussion to several later critics: "And so ends this incongruous drama, a strange union of the spirit of an ancient mystery and of a modern *vaudeville,* but not without poetry, and not more incongruous and more undecorous than the similar dramas which, at the same period, and in other countries, found a place in the princely halls of the most cultivated, and were listened to with edification in monasteries and cathedrals by the most religious."

Spitzer, in his article in *Hispanic Review,* picked up this statement to show that there is a kernel of truth in Ticknor's words, if Ticknor's words are properly interpreted: "Provided that we replace this last term [*vaudeville*], which has semantically deteriorated in our days, by a noble term such as 'light opera' or *Singspiel*, we must acknowledge that Ticknor was right in his definition, if not . . . in his appraisal of the play." "To apply to it the label 'incongruous' is to forget," continues Spitzer, "that in Renaissance Catholicism sensuous delight that appeals to the eye and the ear is not incompatible with the firmest of dogmatic convictions. . . . The *Auto da Sibila Cassandra,* an act of faith made visible on the stage, is what Gundolf has called, in reference to certain Shakespearean plays, a *Weltfeier,* a celebration in which the whole historical world takes part."

For Mia I. Gerhardt, in a careful analysis, *The Play of the Sibyl Cassandra* is "one of the masterpieces of Spanish theater of the sixteenth century." [13] For Miss Gerhardt there is no clash between the comical beginning of the play and the grandeur of the conclusion. This able critic finds real unity in the play and live and animated characters, and she declares that an early scene between Cassandra and Solomon, is one of "fine and just comedy, of a tone both realistic and light, such as the medieval pastoral play hardly knew and such as the Renaissance pastoral play will not find again." The fact that the critics have paid so much attention to this particular play, with varying interpretations and opinions, right down to the mid-twentieth century, is evidence of its significance in the Vicentine totality, where it stands out as a landmark in this type of work, in which, as Spitzer has so rightly said, there exists "no 'hodgepodge' of secular and religious motifs, but a natural growth of the latter out of the former."

In this same Salamancan tradition, as was previously noted, there are two other plays to be mentioned: the mid-career *Play of the Four Seasons* (*Auto dos Quatro Tempos*) and the very late *Play of Mofina Mendes* (*Auto da Mofina Mendes*). Both, like the *Sibyl Cassandra,* accent the glorification of the Virgin Mary rather than the adoration of the Christ-Child, although the two parts of the Nativity celebration are present in them.

V   The Play of the Four Seasons

The Play of the Four Seasons, of some 650 lines, in Spanish, was doubtless presented on a Christmas morning, and probably in 1516 as Bell (*Four Plays,* p. xxii) decides, because of "the superior development of the play's structure and even of its thought, its resemblance to the *Triunfo do Inverno* (1529), the introduction of a French song, of the gods of Greece and of a psalm similar to that in the *Auto da Mofina Mendes* (1534) and the perfection of the metre." Bell admits that in a rougher form the play may have been presented at a much earlier Christmas.

The *Auto dos Quatro Tempos* (text in *Obras completas,* I, 97–125) begins with the announcement by a seraphim to the archangel and to two other angels of the birth of the Christ-Child. This announcement is accompanied by much praise of the Blessed Virgin. The four figures approach the manger, and sing a *vilancete* which is a free adaptation of *Te Deum laudamus* ("We praise Thee, O Lord"). Following this adoration, there come on to the stage the four Seasons: Winter, dressed as a shepherd, alternatively singing and speaking in verse, and complaining about the bad weather; then Spring, who sings and speaks of the joys of Nature's rebirth; then Summer, who speaks of heat and dryness; finally Autumn, who has come to gather the fruits of the year, while berating hot Summer for having ruined the crop. Jupiter interrupts the arguing of the Seasons to announce that in this new dispensation, brought about by the birth of the Messiah, the pagan gods and goddesses have abdicated. He has come in person to present their homage and adoration before the manger. Finally, David, dressed as a shepherd, presents his homage too, by singing and speaking a paraphrase of several songs and a part of the Book of Daniel. *The Four Seasons* then comes to an end with all joining in a joyful singing of *Te Deum laudamus.*

From this brief résumé it can be clearly seen that this play has a close connection with Christmas morning religious celebrations; and that an important, and comical, feature in it is the debate of the four seasons, from which the play draws its name. Especially in the exchange of insults between the four divisions of the year, it points to similar and earlier pastoral argumentation in plays of the Spanish Salamancan School, and also, to the long tradition of the medieval debate of the Seasons. In the combination of the profane and the religious, it is once again, like *The Play of the Sibyl Cassandra,* not an "incongruous" drama, thoughtlessly mixing the secular and the religious, but rather a drama—very proper to its times—in which the divine is shown to be immanent or latent in the most trifling of human affairs. Indeed, in this play, as Spitzer declared for the *Sibyl Cassandra,* we can repeat that "there exists no 'hodgepodge' of secular and religious motifs, but a natural growth of the latter out of the former."

Eugenio Asensio, in his enlightening consideration of the play,[14] points out through the listing of parallel lines that Gil Vicente's unusual show of mythological erudition, here presented through the mouth of Jupiter, was drawn from the fifteenth-century Spaniard Juan de Mena's *Coronación,* and from Juan de Mena's own prose commentaries of the poem, which ran through three editions before 1500.[15] Asensio also notes that the great profusion of astronomical-geographical knowledge poured forth by Jupiter as he presented to the Christ-Child the homage of the Universe was based directly on Bartolomaeus Anglicus' *De proprietatibus rerum,* which had been translated into Spanish by Fray Vicente de Burgos and published in Toulouse in 1494. This "encyclopedia of Shakespeare's," as it has been called on occasion, by Bartholomew of England, to give him his non-Latin name, was widely known, and was an important source of erudition for many writers.[16] As has been seen, Gil Vicente did not fail to use it either.

It is to be recalled that dramatic works by Juan del Encina were presented on Christmas mornings, before the Duke and Duchess of Alba, who had just heard matins in the palace chapel; and in the Portuguese Court, no doubt the audience witnessing *The Play of the Four Seasons* had just recited all or part of the Office of Our Lady for Advent. In the play itself they found a dramatized version of matins and *laudes,* of the *Laudate dominum de caelis;* and of the *Benedicite* of the three youths in the Book of Daniel. These elements formed part of the *laudes* and matins, and were recited together. It is evident that the various scenes of the play form "an organic whole." The angel's *Te Deum;* the mixture of psalms from the Office of Our Lady, in David's mouth; the storm and calm of the Four Seasons; the participation of Jupiter, king of the fallen gods and the deposed lord of the elements—all of these "are combined harmoniously to form a vast perspective of the universe which runs to adore and to acclaim the divine Prince" (Asensio, p. 356). This dramatization had a close connection with the religious service just completed by the royal household, and it was part and parcel of the Christmas religious festival and must be interpreted as such.

In his argument for the year for *The Four Seasons,* Bell had stressed the play's "superior development." Asensio agrees that the play is indeed "the most beautiful perhaps of the *laudes*" in dramatic form. Framing the play are two long recitatives, by the seraphim and David respectively, toward the beginning and toward the end. In between, there is an opera-like effect produced by the many sung portions, which are usually in the short line (eight and four syllables) of the fifteenth-century Spanish Jorge Manrique's *coplas de pie quebrado.* The total effect is an attractive vehicle for the Christmas story: to commemorate the Bethlehem birth of centuries before.

VI   The Play of Mofina Mendes

The *Auto da Mofina Mendes,* whose title might be interpreted as *The Play of the Luckless Miss Mendes,* is in Portuguese, and was acted in a way similar to *The Four Seasons,* on Christmas morning of 1534, in Evora. (The text is to be found in *Obras completas,* I, 127–162.) The King was now João III, at whose birth thirty-two years previously, Gil Vicente had recited the dramatic *Herdsman's Monologue.*

The long opening scene of this play presents a friar who ridicules scholastic friars in a way reminiscent of Erasmus' *Enchiridion* and *Moria.* (No wonder then that this scene was ordered deleted by the *Indices Expurgatorios* of 1586 and 1624.) The friar, after this satirical and comical introduction, proceeds to relate the plot of the play in the manner common to Torres Naharro's dramatic works, with the conventional "introito" and "argumento" (prologue and résumé). The friar relates to the audience that the play about to be seen is really called "The Mysteries of the Virgin," and that it will consist of two parts or mysteries: the Annunciation and the Nativity. In between, however, there will be found a non-sacred section, dealing with the luckless shepherdess Mendes.

When the play proper begins, the Virgin comes on stage dressed as a queen, accompanied by angels, with musical instruments, and four handmaidens: Poverty, Humility, Faith, and Prudence. These maidens are reading prophecies concerning Mary, and at a dramatic moment the Mother of God is saluted by the Angel Gabriel: "Hail, Mary, full of grace. . . ." A curtain is drawn, and a new stage set is presented: shepherds, in a comic interlude, discuss the hapless shepherdess who is continually having misfortunes. Miss Mendes then appears, singing and dancing. She is carrying a jug of olive oil on her head, and, as is to be expected, one more accident befalls her! However, she takes this new misfortune in her stride, and as she departs still singing, she proclaims philosophically that all human fortune, like her jug of oil, will some day crash to the ground and be destroyed.

The shepherds lie down to sleep, and the second, and final, mystery is introduced. There is praise of the Divine Lamb, and the Virgin and her maidens sing a paraphrase of the 148th Psalm: "Praise the Lord on high, / Spirits of the blest! / Praise him in the sky, / His glory ceaselessly / Let your song attest" ("Ó devotas almas felis / Para sempre sem cessar / Laudate Dominum de coelis, / Laudate Eum in excelsis / Quanto se pode louvar.") Joseph and the allegorical figure Faith complain that Mankind, intent on worldly pleasures, will not light the candle of glory, which is being carried around, the Divine Babe cries in the cradle, and the angels awaken the shepherds to move forward to adore Him. The angels then play their musical instruments, the handmaidens sing, the shepherds dance, and the little play comes to an end.

Rustic scenes of pure farce for entertainment's sake, allegorical enrichment for the edification of the faithful, the glorification of the Mother, the adoration of the Son—all are before us in this final after-Matins Christmas play. It is the year 1534, but we are back in the religious milieu of the *Auto Pastoril Castelhano* and of the *Auto dos Reis Magos*. Through this, and through his playful shepherds, Gil Vicente has shown us that he has not forgotten his early masters of the Salamancan School, even after a period of some twenty-five years. In the meantime, however, he had scaled loftier heights in the religious *genre* and had experienced richer dramatic adventures, free from experimentation, from incertitudes and medieval naïveté, having established in the mid-teens his full-fledged Morality play, with his three *Ships* and the *Soul's Journey*.

CHAPTER 4

The Moralities and the Mysteries

I N his three *Ships* and in his *Soul's Journey*, as has been mentioned, Gil Vicente reaches the highest point in his presentation of religious themes on the stage. Here, as I. S. Révah has written (*Hispanic Review*, 1959, p. 190), "he has definitively established the type of the religious Morality." Indeed, in these four allegories the dramatist seems to have been divinely inspired to create masterpieces which have had a lasting significance. For Carolina Michaëlis de Vasconcelos, the three *Ships* constitute "an admirable *Dance Macabre* or popular *Divine Comedy*"; [1] for Bell, the *Soul's Journey* is "a Passion Play," which "in some sense forms a Portuguese pendant" to the Spanish Jorge Manrique's *Couplets on the Death of his Father (Coplas por la muerte de su padre)* and corresponds to "the modern *Stabat* on the eve of Good Friday" (*Four Plays*, p. 73).

I *The Three Ships*

Oscar de Pratt (*Notas e comentários*, p. 190) finds in the *Ships* an extremely profound feeling for Christian religiosity, which results, he insists, from a deeper conception on the part of the dramatist of the Divine Judgment than was ever the case in the literary and plastic allegories which preoccupied the minds of the poets and artists of the Middle Ages. The *Soul's Journey*, too, is held in high esteem by Vicentine critics as bearing "serious comparison with *Everyman / Elckerlijk*" (Keates, *The Court Theatre*, p. 120).

The Morality has been popularly defined as the allegorical representation of the conflict between good and evil, and Vicente's four plays, with their allegorical figures and presentations and their concern with the forces of God and of the Devil, fit this general concept of the *genre*. The first play, chronologically, *The*

Ship of Hell (*Auto da Barca do Inferno*), in Portuguese, was presented at Christmas, 1516; and, according to the rubric of the 1562 *Copilação*, "in the Queen's chamber for the consolation of the very Catholic and holy Queen Dona Maria, while she was suffering from the illness of which she died in 1517." [2] A separate copy of the play, which is preserved in the Biblioteca Nacional of Madrid, and which is believed to have been printed shortly after the date of composition, refers to the play's having been performed for the dowager Queen Leanor and King Manuel. This copy, of great importance in Vicentine studies, and which bears the designation "Morality Play" in its title, has been published in modern times by several critics. [3]

The second *Ship*, *The Ship of Purgatory* (*Auto da Barca do Purgatório*), also in Portuguese, was acted on Christmas morning, 1518, before the new Queen Leanor (who had married King Manuel in November of that year) in the chapel of the Hospital de Todos os Santos, Lisbon; [4] and the third *Ship*, *The Ship of Heaven* (*Auto da Barca da Glória*), in Spanish, was presented before the King and Queen, Manuel and Leanor, during Holy Week, 1519, in a chapel in Almeirim. [5] *The Soul's Journey* (*Auto da Alma*), in spite of the *Copilação's* dating of 1508, has been assigned to the year 1518 by Braamcamp Freire, and his date and his arguments have been accepted by Bell (*Four Plays*, p. xxii). [6] This later date has been preferred because of "the maturity and perfection of this beautiful play," and because Lucas Fernández's *Passion Play* (*Auto de la Pasión*), of 1514, may have been before Gil Vicente as he wrote this other morality play in the midst of writing the three *Ships*.

The plot, in brief, of the three *Ships* is the acceptance or rejection, by the ships of Heaven and Hell, of the souls of men as they arrive to cross over the waters to reward or to punishment. The ship of Hell accepts, since the angel's boat to Paradise rejects them, persons of many ranks and positions in life: a gentleman (of pomp and pride), a usurer (with his heavy purse), a cobbler (with the tricks of his trade), a friar (with earthly vices), a procuress (condemned in spite of her "services" to young men and maidens), a Jew (the non-believer), a judge (for accepting bribes), a public prosecutor (for misappropriating state funds), and a hanged man (for sins against society). Into the angel's boat

are accepted a fool (for there was no malice in his sin) and four
noblemen, knights of the Order of Christ, who died for the Faith
in North Africa. To them, as the play comes to an end, the angel
sings:

> Knights of God!
> For you I wait,
> You who fighting met your fate
> For the Christ, the Lord of Heaven:
> From all evil are you free,
> Holy are you certainly;
> Unto him who in such conflict
> Dies eternal peace is given.
>
> (Bell, p. 43)

> (Ó cavaleiros de Deos,
> a vós estou esperando;
> que morrestes pelejando
> por Christo, Senhor dos ceos.
> Sois livres de todo o mal,
> sanctos por certo sem falha,
> que quem morre em tal batalha
> merece paz eternal.)
>
> (*Obras completas,* II, 81–82)

The Ship of Purgatory, "which deals with peasants" (to use the
words of the rubric of the *Copilação*), presents a group of persons
who must purge their guilt along the stream until God deems it
fitting for them to be transported to Heaven: a farmer (who has
moved boundary stones), a market-woman (who has watered
milk), a shepherd (who has tried to seduce a shepherdess), and a
shepherdess (for minor failings). A gambler, however, who has
spurned and cursed the Queen of Heaven, is not given the oppor-
tunity to sojourn on Purgatory's shore, with the certainty of being
taken, in due time, into the angel's boat. The gambler and blas-
phemer can never be redeemed, and, very dramatically, the devils
leap from their boat, grab him, and carry him off. An innocent
young child, however, is taken amid joyful singing into the angel's
boat for Paradise.

The Ship of Heaven deals with "persons of high rank," who are brought in, one by one, by Death. Their many sins are recounted in detail, as they discuss their future with the Devil, the ferryman of Hell, and the angel, the ferryman of Heaven. In turn the failings of a Count, a Duke, a King, an Emperor, a Bishop, an Archbishop, a Cardinal, and even a Pope, are dissected and analysed, much to their detriment, and it is very uncertain whether they will ever gain eternal life. As these high personages present their prayers, their pleas, and their petitions to the Almighty, in their efforts to justify themselves and to escape the Devil's boat, their future hangs in the balance. In fact, the angel tells them all that their evil lives have won for them nothing but eternal punishment, and that their petitions have not been heard. As the angels unfurl their sails to leave them behind, the petitioners kneel down, for on the main sail is painted a crucifix. As the angels' boat pushes off, the Pope, the Emperor, the King, the Cardinal, the Duke, the Archbishop, the Count, and the Bishop, in that order, all pray to the risen Christ. While the angels still pay no attention to their lamentations, the Redeemer does arrive, to take them with him.

II   The Soul's Journey

The Soul's Journey is a "pilgrim's progress," as the Soul of Man travels through the World, tempted by the Devil, but fortunately having for her assistance and guidance her guardian angel; and for her repose and refreshment amid the trials and tribulations of life, the Holy Mother Church. The Soul is a headstrong creature, enjoying free will and often straying from the straight and narrow path at the Devil's bidding into materialism and sin, to return, however, at the end of the allegory, to ways of right and salvation.

As can be seen from a brief consideration of the plots of the *Ships* and of *The Soul's Journey*, Gil Vicente was meditating in dramatic form on matters of life and death, of salvation and damnation, within the framework of Roman Catholic orthodoxy. Eugenio Asensio has studied at some length the sources of the *Ships,* and various critics, above all I. S. Révah, have drawn our attention to literary and live inspiration which must have been before Gil Vicente as he conceived his *Soul's Journey.* Asensio's penetrating article points out that investigation into sources "is situated midway between intellectual history and literary analysis, between studies of culture and of structure," and it is Asensio's purpose in this particular case to pin down and to enlarge upon the vague information already in existence about the sources of the *Ships,* especially the first one, and to analyse some of the processes employed by Gil Vicente in making use of his source materials.[7] Révah, with rare intuition, has been able to analyse Vicente's processes of composition from bookish and live aids at hand.[8]

Even Greek literature played a part in the conception of the first *Ship* through the tenth *Dialogue of the Dead* of Lucian of Samosata, who was extremely popular in Portugal, in Latin translation, in the late fifteenth and early sixteenth centuries. This influence upon Gil Vicente had been noted by several critics, including Paulo Quintela in his edition noted above. In Lucian and in Gil Vicente we have the dead persons arriving at the river, laden with the symbols of their earthly vices, entering into a discussion with Hell's ferryman, and lamenting loudly when it is decided that they must go with him. Also, to the medieval Spanish *Dance of Death* (*Danza de la muerte*) the first two *Ships* have a slight indebtedness. But the third *Ship,* however, in which Death appears in person—and it is only in this third part that Death does so—owes a great deal to the Spanish forerunner, which was being widely read in Gil Vicente's time and was readily available to him. The Spanish *Dance of Death* provides the personages of high rank (the Pope, Emperor, Cardinal, King, etc.), and they enter into a discussion with Death, exactly as they do in Gil Vicente's *Ship of Heaven.* This is indeed Gil Vicente's own "Dance of Death," and in spite of the fact that the Portuguese dramatist has transferred to his other two *Ships* some of the characters of the Spanish *Dance,* it is for the third part of the trilogy that he must have had his model vividly before him as he wrote.

The question has been raised on occasion as to whether Dante's *Divine Comedy* had any influence, direct or indirect, on the *Ships.* Although Paulo Quintela thought not, G. C. Rossi has found continuing echoes of the Italian poem in Gil Vicente's plays.[9] Asensio too, in this difficult matter of the genesis of a work of literature, is inclined to find at least "tenuous echoes" of the *Divine Comedy* and of commentaries on it, which might very well have come to Gil Vicente's attention through the Pedro Fernández de Villegas translation of the *Inferno* which was published in Burgos in 1515.

Teófilo Braga found in the idea of the "ships" the maritime character of the Portuguese people, who had been so ship-conscious over so many years.[10] And Braga reminds us also that Prince Duarte in his *Loyal Counsellor (Leal Conselheiro)*, of the fifteenth century, prepared the way for Gil Vicente with a ship motif. Gil Vicente may indeed have dramatized this traditional theme to which Dom Duarte had given form. There is comparatively little reference in Gil Vicente's works to the glorious maritime discoveries of the day (*The Play of India* is a minor exception), and in the *Ships* there are only two pertinent allusions: Brazil is mentioned by name in the second *Ship*, and in the first, the Devil states that the readied ship is departing for the "Lost Isle," which may here be interpreted as Hell. But "there is perhaps a germ of truth in Braga's idea," comments Asensio. "The author and his public, impregnated with nautical culture, were internally prepared to feel and relive the symbols of the sea, supplied in abundance by the founders of the Christian Faith, men who were accustomed to sea voyages and shipwrecks." As for Gil Vicente's knowing, or not, Dom Duarte's *Leal Conselheiro* and its motif of the two ships (of sin and of virtue), it can only be concluded that this presentation in the two Portuguese authors may be parts of a common theological tradition, with any direct influence completely uncertain.

Into these ecclesiastical influences there enters once again most certainly a book which was extremely popular at that time, as has been stated previously in a discussion of source material of other Vicentine plays: the *Vita Christi* of Ludolphus de Saxonia, in its Spanish translation by Ambrosio Montesino, Alcalá de Henares, 1502. This *Life of Christ* had its ship of Heaven, with its angelic crew. "I imagine," writes Asensio, "that from this work, Gil Vicente took the nucleus of his story, combining the symbols of the Carthusian [Ludolphus of Saxony] with other allegorical fragments."

It is I. S. Révah, as was noted above, who has presented a splendid account of the sources of *The Soul's Journey*. Quoting the introductory prose explanation given at the beginning of the play in the *Copilação,*

As it was very necessary that there should be inns upon the roads for the repose and refreshment of weary wayfarers, so it was fitting that in this transitory life there should be an innkeeper for the refreshment and rest of the souls that go journeying to the everlasting abode of God. This innkeeper of souls is the Holy Mother Church . . . ,

Révah is able to point out that the parallel to a passage in Ludolphus de Saxonia's *Vita Christi* is very striking:

And it says that he carried him to the inn to signify that he put him under the protection of the Holy Church, wherein he placed him, and where, casting aside the burden of sin, every traveller, however tired he may be, is well refreshed, and thus consoled by health-giving sustenance, is refurbished in everything.[11]

The Biblical source of this commentary in the *Vita Christi* is, of course, the Parable of the Good Samaritan (St. Luke X, 30–37), in which "A certain man went down from Jerusalem to Jericho, and fell among robbers, who also stripped him, and having wounded him went away, leaving him half dead. . . ." The Samaritan, we remember, "going up to him, bound up his wounds, pouring in oil and wine: and setting him upon his own beast, brought him to an inn, and took care of him." In *The Soul's Journey*, the Soul has indeed "fallen among thieves," and she is heavy laden with the ornaments and jewels with which the Devil has tempted her to lead her from the straight and narrow path into ways of perdition. Fortunately her good Samaritan, her guardian angel, guides her to an inn, the Holy Mother Church, where good care is taken of her and where she is led to a mystical repast (the emblems of the Passion), served by the learned doctors of the Church, St. Augustine, St. Jerome, St. Ambrose, and St. Thomas. The Soul needs little further bidding to cast aside her finery (the sins, the vanity, and the materialism of the World) and she enters into a spiritual victory, won through faith and good works, which leads to the mansions of the blest.

To recapitulate: in *The Soul's Journey*, the Soul's turning from God to a defiance of Him is the man's going down from Jerusalem to Jericho (from the state of grace to sin) in the Parable of the Good Samaritan. The Soul's yielding to the temptation of the Devil is the falling among thieves. The good Samaritan, as noted above, who saves the traveler through his compassion, in Gil Vicente becomes, through the influence of Ludolphus de Saxonia's *Life of Christ,* the guardian angel, or perhaps Jesus Christ himself, who puts evil to flight and reestablishes the Soul in her former pristine state. The whole kernel of this morality play is, as can be seen, before Gil Vicente in the *Vita Christi,* and Gil Vicente has made excellent use of it, but he has, nevertheless, introduced some modifications from other sources. The struggle between the angel and the devil for the soul of Man was a very common theme in the Middle Ages, and we remember that by this time Gil Vicente had already produced his first *Ship,* in which the souls of dead individuals are taken by either the forces of evil or of good, although the angels and the devil are not really fighting to get them, but it is rather the soul itself struggling and arguing to be accepted in the preferred position. The presence of the learned doctors of the Church in *The Soul's Journey* may have been inspired by contemporary art; and Ludolphus de Saxonia's elements of the Sacrament for a mystical meal have become, in the Vicentine play, the instruments of the Passion: covered by the towel which covered the face of the Crucified Jesus (the veronica) are the scourge, the crown of thorns, the nails of the cross, and the Crucifix itself. In very moving words the doctors adore and pray to these elements, and the total effect of the play, from the beginning to the ending, is one of high dramatic and lyrical significance.

The lyrical value of these moralities—and Gil Vicente's fine contribution as a lyric poet in his plays will be recapitulated in a later chapter—should be particularly mentioned at this point. Going from the general poetic impression of these four plays, which is one of high caliber, into concrete examples, one might point to the song of the four knights, a song in four parts, at the end of *The Ship of Hell:* "To the Ship, the Ship of Salvation" ("À barca, à barca segura") and to the song of the three angels, carrying oars, at the beginning of *The Ship of Purgatory:* "Rowers now are rowing / a ship of great delight." ("Remando vão remadores / barca de grande alegria"). Likewise the unprinted song of the five angels at the beginning of *The Ship of Heaven* must have enchanted the audience. In *The Soul's Journey* most striking are the Latin chants of the four venerable doctors of the

Church, as they kneel, and adore, as has been mentioned, the elements of the Passion: before the dishes containing these elements they sing "Vexilla regis prodeunt"; before the veronica which covers them: "Salve sancta Facies"; before the scourge, "Ave flagellum"; before the crown of thorns, "Ave corona spinarum"; before the wood and nails of the cross, "Dulce lignum, dulcis clavis"; and before the Crucifix itself, "Domine Jesu Christe." Then, with a final "Te Deum laudamus," they all go off the stage to adore the Tomb and end the play.

Within the *Ships*, the "Lessons" and the "Responses" of *The Ship of Heaven* are most moving for an audience in tune with the beliefs and practices of the Roman Catholic Church. "O spare me, O God, for my days are but vanity," cries the Count, as he, in a mixture of Latin and Spanish, paraphrases the Office of the Dead. "Thy hands, O Lord, created me," intones the Duke, as he too makes use of the Office of the Dead, and of the Book of Job. "My soul is weary of my life," laments the King as he imitates Juan del Encina and Garci Sánchez de Badajoz, who before him had imitated the Book of Job and the liturgical *Requiem,* and continues on to a response from the Office of the Dead: "Remember me, O God, I pray, my past sins." The Emperor's "Lesson" from Job, "O that Thou wouldest hide me in the grave," is complemented by a "Response" paraphrasing the same Book: "O Lord, deliver me from death, the eternal strife, for in Thee had I always faith."

Through the Bishop, Archbishop, Cardinal, and Pope, Gil Vicente presents additional Lessons and Responses, based on Job, Chapters XIII and XIV. Many theological writers before him had made use of this material, which had entered into the liturgy of the Office of the Dead, and Gil Vicente makes moving and effective use of it once more. "Answer me Thou, O Lord," complains the Bishop. "Why hast Thou turned away Thy face? . . . Remember that my life is but wind, and my eyes shall not return to see good things. . . ." The Archbishop similarly laments: "My spirit, O Lord, is spent; my days have reached their end and sadness and the tomb are upon me." But in his Response, he can say in triumph with Job: "For I know that my Redeemer liveth, and in the last day I shall rise out of the earth. Because He is my Savior, I in Him shall be saved." But it is the Cardinal who intones with Job the main theme of the *Ships:* "Man born of woman, living for a short time, is filled with many miseries. . . . He cometh forth like a flower, and is destroyed, and fleeth as a shadow. . . . I have sinned, what shall I do to Thee, O Keeper of men?"

The Pope is chided by Death, as he brings him in after the others for having deemed himself immortal, not having given a thought to the possible ending of life. The Devil welcomes him as one who has indulged in worldliness and lust. Simony and deceit have been his crimes also, and he has not done his Christian duty, which was to set a good example for his people. As Marques Braga reminds us (*Obras completas,* II, 164, note to line 6), we can almost hear Erasmus saying in his *Stultitiae Laus* of 1509: "The popes do not think that the worst enemies of the Church are the bad popes who shamefully traffic in their favors, who corrupt doctrine through forced interpretations and destroy it entirely through the contagious example of abominable intemperance." The Pope, then, in *The Ship of Heaven,* is most amazed and terrified to be in danger of eternal damnation, and he repents of his worldliness. "Why," he asks pitifully, with Job and the Office of the Dead, "didst Thou bring me forth out of the womb? Thou hast put me on Thy throne and made me Thy shepherd on earth. Better it would have been that I had not been born!" Then throwing himself in his "Response" upon God's mercy, he begs for compassion and forgiveness, as the threatening devil tries to make him embark for Hell. As mentioned before, it is only through the appearing of Christ that even this great figure of the Church is saved.

Marques Braga (*Obras completas,* II, 169), quoting Oliveira Martins,[12] meditates upon this treatment of the highest personage of the Church: "It is true that in the end they are all saved. In the presence of the Court, before which the *Auto* was performed, the opposite was not possible. But they are saved how? With the coming of Christ, and holding fast to the oars, which are the wounds of the Redeemer. The supreme sacrifice of God is necessary to remit the crimes of the mighty." Keates (*The Court Theatre,* p. 122) suggests that this Divine intervention "is perhaps intentionally ambiguous: the sins of those in high places are great indeed if a special second redemption is needed to cancel them."

Whatever the theological or sociological explanation may be, this presentation of the mighty, and their treatment at the hands of the dramatist, shows that Gil Vicente was in a firm position at Court to have handled so boldly the most prominent backsliding servants of the Church; and he did it, it is to be observed, through their reactions to the situation, in a most dramatic and poetic way.

This reference to the personages of *The Ship of Heaven* brings to mind the whole gallery of portraits in the trilogy of the *Ships*. The tripartite division of late-medieval Portuguese society ("middle class," commoners, and persons of high estate) is here before us in a very vivid fashion, and each character, as he or she passes before us, is sufficiently well portrayed to imprint his or her personality upon our minds. This characterization, however, is of one piece, for it is born of "the unchanging attitude that [the character] has created during life, and which he is unable to cast off in death" (Keates, p. 121). Each person, as has been mentioned before, usually has with him (or her) an accompanying "prop" closely connected with the major failing: the idle gentleman of *The Ship of Hell*, for example, has with him his chair and his page to carry it. The aforementioned *editio princeps* (1517?) of the play includes an illustration of the *fidalgo* arriving at the quay off which ride the ships of Hell and Heaven; and behind him comes the page bearing his long train and the chair he always wanted for his ease. The usurer, of the same play, has his purse; the cobbler his lasts; the friar wields his sword for fencing and leads his girl friend by the hand! Brigida Vaz, the procuress, a descendant of Spain's great Celestina of some twenty years before, has with her the tricks of her trade, and a Jew enters carrying a goat on his back. Celso Láfer, in his recent penetrating monograph,[13] analyses this situation, and concludes that Gil Vicente is presenting the image of the Jew carrying the sins of the World. At the end of this episode the Jew cannot even be taken into the ship of Hell, but, with his goat, must be towed behind. This Láfer takes to be the Wandering Jew, who has in him both a diabolical obstinacy and an expiatory function: the last to be saved will be the Jews and the salvation of the Jews will mean the salvation of all of Humanity.

António J. Saraiva pays particular attention to the fool (the *parvo*), who plays a very special rôle in *The Ship of Hell*, in that he comments on the action which relates to the other characters of the play.[14] Of the Jew, the fool says, for example, "Did he not insult the dead / In the churchyard overhead? / Was not meat served at his board / On the feast-days of the Lord?" (Bell, p. 35) ("E s'elle mijou nos finados / no adro de San Gião! / E comia a carne da panella / no dia de nosso Senhor."—*Obras completas,* II, 69). In other words, the *parvo* is a crown witness for and against (usually against) the plaintiffs as they present their pleas and excuses and have their sins assessed in this court case which decides their ultimate destinies. "The *parvo,*" to use Laurence Keates' words once again, "helps wonderfully to bind the separate scenes together."

The characters of the second *Ship* are just as fascinating as those of the first: as an example of a person with the instrument of his trade is the farmer carrying a plow on his back. As the finest example, from this *Ship,* of a delightful female character is Marta Gil, the market-woman, who as Bell has noted (*The Ship of Hell,* pp. 11–12) "may be met unchanged today." "There seems to have been considerable doubt," continues Bell, "as to even the ultimate salvation of Marta Gil; but she proved really one too many for the Devil. Nothing escapes her, she sees at a glance that his boat is stranded and is quick to take advantage. It is one of the delightful character touches that Marta, who has an amazing flow of language at her command, and has not allowed the Devil to get in a word edgeways, complains that he is so talkative!" These persons, and others, are before the audience in the second *Ship;* and in the third there are the personages of high estate, to whom sufficient reference has already been made.

It seems to be historically true that it was the benign influence of the dowager Queen Leanor which inspired Gil Vicente to write these very fine and very elevating plays in the last years of her life. And it seems to be historically true also that João III was guilty of turning Gil Vicente away from these religious interests when he came to the throne in 1521. For João III, as can be seen from the chronology of dramatic activity, kept his court dramatist very busy with lighter court entertainment over a period of several years following his accession. Nevertheless, the important and outstanding moralities which have just been discussed were followed by significant religious plays from time to time in Gil Vicente's later period. Three plays which may be called "mystery plays," in that "the conflict between Good and Evil is treated historically rather than metaphysically" (Keates, p. 123), are *The Play of the History of God* (*Auto da História de Deus*, or *Breve Sumário da História de Deus*), *The Dialogue on the Resurrection* (*Diálogo sôbre a Ressurreição*), and *The Play of the Canaanite Woman* (*Auto da Cananeia*), of the years 1527, 1528, and 1534, respectively. These three, along with the moralities and other religious plays mentioned elsewhere, are important contributions made by Gil Vicente to the history of theological drama.

III   The History of God

The History of God (the Portuguese text is to be found in *Obras completas*, II, 171–215) portrays the destinies of Mankind from the Creation to the Redemption. At the beginning of the play, which the *Copilação*'s rubric says was performed before João III and Queen Catarina in Almeirim in 1527, an angel announces to the members of the audience, by way of introduction, that they will see old things reincarnated, for those things are always worth telling. And since "the Resurrection of our Lord has its roots in the orchard, where Adam fell into sin," it is well to start at the beginning of things. Therefore, the first scene after the introductory lines shows Lucifer, the prince of devils, holding court and planning an all-out war against God. Satan, a member of the inner Council, is sent to tempt Adam and Eve. Another devil, Belial, very humanly and very humorously, is extremely jealous of the preference shown a rival, especially on Satan's successful return; and especially when Lucifer rewards Satan by making him captain of the powers of evil in the world, to work on the descendents of the first parents.

The stage then portrays an angel, carrying a clock, and with her World, dressed like a king, and Time, World's overseer. In this allegory, since sin is temporal and the kindness of God is infinite, the angel orders World to show Adam and Eve some favor. They, repentant, come on to the stage to praise God for his mercy. At this Abel, a shepherd, the friend of God and a good servant, sings the beautiful "Worship, O mountains / The God unseen" ("Adorae montanhas / O Deus das alturas")—Bell, *Lyrics of Gil Vicente*, No. 8, pp. 16–17; *Obras completas*, II, 185. Death then carries Abel off to Limbus, and he is followed on the stage by Job, who rejects Satan's temptation, declaring, in the words used by the Archbishop in *The Ship of Heaven*, "For I know that my Redeemer liveth, and in the last day I shall rise out of the earth. Because He is my Savior, I in Him shall be saved." Satan, in despair, touches him and turns him into a leper. Then follow, in the mouth of Job, many quotations from the Book of Job and from the Office of the Dead, very reminiscent indeed of the lessons and responses of *The Ship of Heaven*, such as the Pope's "Why didst Thou bring me forth out of the womb? . . . Better it would have been that I had not been born!"

In this first part of the play, the four patriarchs (Adam, Eve, Abel, and Job) represent the "Law of Nature." In the second part, the "Law of Scripture," as World explains to the audience, is represented by Moses, Isaiah, David, and Abraham. Abraham, on stage, praises God, the Eternal Spirit, the Creator of Souls; Moses praises God, the Creator of the World; David proclaims that the most acceptable sacrifice to Him is a contrite heart; and Isaiah predicts that the Messiah will be born in Bethlehem of Judea of a Virgin. A third part, representing the "Law of Grace," presents St. John, who proclaims to mortals, "Behold the Lamb of God who taketh away the sins of the World." St. John's request of Death is granted: that he be taken from Earth to Limbus to visit the prisoners there, "whose captivity soon will come to an end."

The stage next depicts the arrival of St. John in Limbus. The prisoners there sing a beautiful Spanish ballad, which, the *Copilação* relates, "the author himself composed for the purpose": "The prisoners were lamenting, / For a long time they had been weeping, / In a sad dark prison, / Suffering and sighing. . . ." ("Voces daban prisioneros, / luengo tiempo están llorando, / en triste cárcel escura / padeciendo y suspirando. . . .)"—*Obras completas*, II, 204. But very aware of their plight are the Lord of the World and his blessed Mother, who has conceived of the Holy Spirit and given birth to the Christ Child. He will grow up and suffer death on the Cross, the ballad goes on to relate, to redeem the unfortunate. Then the Redeemer does appear on stage, and homage is paid to Him by World, Time, and Death. He speaks, declaring that His kingdom is not of this world, and that He will be crucified for the sins of mankind.

Meanwhile Lucifer is very upset by the Christ-Redeemer's presence in the World, for Lucifer looks upon him as a "dangerous element." This devil tempts Christ to perform miracles, and goes on to offer Him the whole world if He will bow down and worship him. Refusing these worldly honors, Christ sets His face toward Jerusalem, where He knows that the Cross is waiting for Him. As the devils are overwhelmed by terror and sickness—"even my finger nails are yellow," laments Belial—the scene changes to a tomb with the dead Christ. Then amid trumpets and singing, the play comes to an end as Christ appears in Resurrection, entering Limbus to free the prisoners held therein.

"The *História de Deus* may best be described as a Harrowing of Hell," states Keates (*The Court Theatre,* p. 123); and this is quite true, for the very last words of the play, against the triumphant background of the Resurrection, are formed by the pitiful laments of Belial and Satan, who address their king Lucifer to warn him of the mortal danger to the Cause of Darkness. "It is also," continues Keates, "a chronicle of the Three Laws and (the reason for its classification as a mystery) a *résumé* of Old Testament history." And one could go farther, to add that it is really in addition a history of the New Testament for it includes the essence of the New Dispensation in its "Law of Grace." Indeed the drama, which is not any longer than the usual Vicentine court play, compresses theological history in an amazing way to reach a unity of expression which is outstanding. The audience assembled to be edified on the occasion of the play's *début* surely did receive, in a manner vigorously conceived and executed, a recapitulation of theological history in capsule form, and many lessons on which to ponder.

In tune with this grandiose subject matter and the solemn treatment of it, is a verse form which appears in this play for the first time in Gil Vicente: a twelve-syllable line, with its hemistich (of six syllables), in varied combinations which are rhythmic and harmonious in the handling. Gil Vicente, as is well known, was most fond of the short line of eight syllables (with its hemistich of four syllables), but here he has attempted, very skilfully, a new metrical form, with splendid results. The early *Auto de S. Martinho* had used the twelve-syllable line, it is true, in lyric stanzas in imitation of Juan del Encina, but this late *History of God*, using twelve and six syllable lines in an agile mixture, reveals a considerable improvement and development forward in versification as a comparison of the two dramatic pieces will prove.

IV   The Dialogue on the Resurrection

The short *Dialogue on the Resurrection* (1528) follows closely in time and in theme the preceding play. (The Portuguese text is to be found in *Obras completas*, II, 217–232). Three rabbis are commenting on the events of the Crucifixion, and on the "unfortunate Messiah" who now, they think, is buried and finished, along with all of His hopes and promises. Then very dramatically two centurions, who were guarding the tomb, report in amazement that "He is risen." Amid much discussion and consternation, the rabbis can only conclude that if He is really risen it will be the end of their religion. Their decision is that they must go forward pretending that all is well, and not admit defeat to any living soul.

It is worth while noting that Gil Vicente does very well in his characterization of the three Jewish protagonists, Levi, Samuel, and Aroz. A great deal of his success lies in his imitation of the Jewish "accent" in Portuguese as he observed it round about him (see Teyssier, *La Langue de Gil Vicente*, pp. 199–226). Whereas *The History of God* was a play majestic in its gravity and solemnity, this *Dialogue* is farcical in treatment, and it is the Jews who bear the brunt of the ridicule, for they are hypocritical and unlikeable. Generally speaking, Gil Vicente showed great tolerance and sympathy for non-Christians (as, for example, in his letter of 1531 to João III, discussed in a later chapter), but in his religious plays the intolerance and religious fervor, typical of early sixteenth-century Portugal, is normally very evident. The Jew in this play (see Celso Láfer, p. 49) is the contemporary Portuguese Jew who will not accept the proof of Scripture, and it is against him that the anti-Semitism of the Nation is directed in this *Dialogue*. The conception is certainly medieval, without a ray of Renaissance enlightenment falling upon it. Of the play as a whole, Keates says in conclusion: "It is easy to dismiss [*The Dialogue*] as of little dramatic value, but it is in fact a graphic vignette of imaginary events immediately after the Resurrection. It bears comparison with anything done since in its genre."

V   The Play of the Canaanite Woman

The Play of the Canaanite Woman (*Auto da Cananeia*), whose Portuguese-Spanish text is to be found in *Obras completas*, II, 233–264, was written at the request of the Abbess of Ouvidelas, and was acted in her convent near Lisbon, in 1534. Although several critics have said that the play is based on St. Mark, VII, 25–30 ("For a woman, as soon as she heard of him, whose daughter had an unclean spirit, came in and fell down at his feet. For the woman was a Gentile, a Syrophenician born. . . . And when she was come into her house, she found the girl lying upon the bed, and that the devil was gone out."), it is very clear from the title of the play, and other circumstances, that Gil Vicente was using the version in St. Matthew, XV, 22–28 ("And behold a woman of Canaan who came out of those coasts, crying out, said to him: Have mercy on me, O Lord, thou Son of David: my daughter is grievously troubled by a devil. . . . Then Jesus answering, said to her: O woman, great is thy faith: be it done to thee as thou wilt: and her daughter was cured from that hour.") In detail, both the St. Matthew version and the play include the intercession of the disciples, which element is missing in St. Mark.

The Play of the Canaanite Woman begins with a pastoral prologue, which presents three shepherdesses who both sing and speak in verse. The first, Silvestra, represents the "Law of Nature," and her task is to guard the flock of pagans; the second, Hebreia, representing the "Law of Scripture," looks after the flock of Jews; and the third, Veredina, the "Law of Grace," cares for the sheep of the Redeemer. This Redeemer, announces Veredina, has come to Earth and is going about preaching, teaching, and declaring the divine prophecies. Satan and Beelzebub, in a discussion on stage, reveal that Christ has rejected all temptation (a reference back to *The History of God*); and right now, declares Beelzebub, the Canaanite woman is seeking His aid to cast out Beelzebub's possession of her daughter.

At this point on to the stage come Christ and six apostles: St. Peter, St. John, St. James, St. Philip, St. Andrew, and St. Simon. They are asking the Master how to pray. With a pure and contrite heart, answers Jesus, you should pray in this manner:

Pater noster qui es in coelis, sanctificetur nomen tuum. Adveniat regnum tuum, fiat voluntas tua, sicut in coelo et in terra. Panem nostrum quotidianum da nobis hodie et dimitte nobis debita nostra, sicut et nos dimittimus debitoribus nostris, e ne nos inducas in tentationem, sed libera nos a malo. Amen.

Christ's commentary on the prayer is interrupted by the arrival of the Canaanite woman, who, like the shepherdesses of the early scenes of the play, alternately sings and speaks in verse. Her plea that Jesus should help her daughter is supported by the Apostles. Even when Jesus says, "I was not sent but to the sheep that are lost of the house of Israel" (St. Matthew, XV, 24), the apostles continue their entreaties, with a comical interruption from Beelzebub: "It's none of your business!" At the end of this rather long scene, which becomes a verbal debate between the disciples and Beelzebub, the Canaanite woman re-states her petition, and Jesus, moved to compassion by her perseverance and faith, performs the miracle, *in absentia.*

Beelzebub carries the "bad" news to Satan, and the devils are amazed that Jesus did not even have to visit the ailing daughter, nor move from where he was. At Christ's "Ite, maledicti Patris mei!", Beelzebub relates, all of the devils within the girl had to hurriedly depart. The devils are left, as they were in *The History of God,* most pessimistic about any future success on their part ("because this Man is eternal"); and the play ends with the Canaanite woman's rendering praise and thanks to the Redeemer, and St. Peter's answering in the name of the disciples and calling all to adore the Master.

This play, which has been edited by Agostinho de Campos (Lisbon, 1938), has in it, as has been noted, many reminiscences of *The History of God.* The central theme in *The Play of the Canaanite Woman,* however, as Pierre David has pointed out,[15] is the exemplification of the power of the Lord's Prayer, when properly applied with perseverance, faith, and understanding. It is true that the Biblical books do not connect the Lord's Prayer (St. Matthew, VI) with the episode of the woman of Canaan, but Gil Vicente's play preserves its unity by making the casting out of the devils an effective use of this prayer of intercession. The Portuguese Church of Gil Vicente's time, explains Pierre David, in its "Roman-Frank" rite, included in its Lesson for the second Sunday in Lent the Evangel of the Canaanite Woman (instead of the Evangel of the Transfiguration); and this Evangel of the Canaanite Woman "furnished the central theme of the remainder of the Mass and of the Office." Therefore David, in his helpful article, is able to show clearly why the Abbess of Ouvidelas had asked of Gil Vicente a play on that subject, and for the very day in question, which was March 1, in 1534.

Georges Le Gentil feels that Gil Vicente knew in some way or other some of the medieval French mystery plays.[16] Le Gentil is quite certain that Vicente had surely read or had heard read some of the Picard texts of the *mystères* current in his day (it is to be recalled that Gil Vicente seems to have had some knowledge of French, in that he uses that language to some extent, as has been seen, in *The Play of Faith*, and in *The Play of the Fairies*). As a specific influence, Le Gentil points to the fact that the hierarchy of devils (Lucifer, then Satan, etc.) is the same in the work of the Portuguese dramatist as in the French mystery plays of the Middle Ages. And the French critic graciously concludes that Gil Vicente has produced an improvement over the French, agreeing with Agostinho de Campos that *The Play of the Canaanite Woman* "is much better written and better constructed" than the French mystery plays. It is indeed gratifying to have the international recognition that, through concentration of interest and sure dramatic instinct, the Portuguese writer, almost at the end of his dramatic career, produced for a specific occasion in a specific place one of his most satisfying works of the religious *genre*. *The Play of the Canaanite Woman, The Play of the History of God*, and even the slighter *Dialogue on the Resurrection*, along with the superior *Ships* and his *Soul's Journey*, have indeed proved Gil Vicente's abilities in the field.

CHAPTER 5

The Farces and the Comedies

WHEN in the 1508–1509 period Gil Vicente turned back with vigor from his goldsmith's activities to theater, and entered the realm of farce and comedy in general, he was entering a *genre* in which he would be very prolific and very successful. From the first of his farces, *Who Has Bran?* (*Quem Tem Farelos?*) and *The Play of India* (*Auto da India*), of a realistic nature, to the final Vicentine play, *The Forest of Deceits* (*Floresta de Enganos*) of 1536, which is "comedy" of a fantastic nature, this type of play would constitute a major contribution to Court entertainment and to the enrichment of the theatrical tradition.

Certainly Gil Vicente did not simply draw farce and comedy from a hat, and present it to his audience. As has been indicated in a previous chapter, there were forerunners of the comic *genre* in the Portuguese Middle Ages and even in Gil Vicente's own time; and Gil Vicente was a keen observer of literary and live phenomena. He made good use of all that had been before him and of all that was around him, and his outstanding talent stood him in good stead in many realms of artistic endeavor; farce and comedy being only one of them.

Who Has Bran? has been assigned to December, 1508, or January, 1509, by Braamcamp Freire, and *The Play of India* to 1509. *Who Has Bran?* is in a mixture of Portuguese and Spanish, but *The Play of India* is in Portuguese only. Here, using his native language exclusively in a play for the first time, Gil Vicente seems to be freeing himself from his Spanish literary "masters," although, as we know, he returned to them for inspiration throughout his whole dramatic career.

I Who Has Bran?

Quem Tem Farelos? (the text is to be found in *Obras completas*, V, 57–88) has been called a sketch of national customs, and "in its

gaiety and concentration [is] perhaps the best of the farces"
(Bell, *Gil Vicente*, p. 50). Other titles by which the play has
been known are "The Farce of the Squires" ("Farsa dos Escu-
deiros") or "The Farce of the Poor Squire" ("Farsa do Escudeiro
Pobre"), titles which are very closely connected with the plot. *O
Auto da India* (the text is to be found in *Obras completas*, V,
89–166) is a reflection of the influence of the discovery of India on
the home life of the Portuguese; but the treatment is farcical, not
historical, as the full title indicates: "Farce Called the Play of
India" ("Farsa Chamada o Auto da India"). The very curious title
"Who Has Bran?" arises from the opening scene in which two
servants, of two different squires, enter the stage asking "Who has
bran?" for their mules. Variety is provided in that one servant
speaks Portuguese and one Spanish. The two servants discuss
their masters: one is a poet and musician, sighing over his Lady,
but never paying his bills; the other is described as being presumptuous, talkative, and foolish, taking over two hours to dress,
and, in addition, never paying his bills either.

In due time we meet the first squire, Aires Rosado, who is reading a poem of the *Cancioneiro* style, which he has written to his
Lady. Later the scene changes, and Aires Rosado is outside Isabel's window, where he serenades her with playing and singing,
amid the barking of dogs, the meowing of cats, and the crowing
of roosters. To add to the farcical confusion out comes Isabel's
mother to drive the suitor away and scold her daughter.

II   The Play of India

It is clear that we are in the realm of the continuing tradition of
medieval farce. Almost slapstick in its presentation, the words of
the servants, the actions of the love-sick poet-squire, the quarrelling of the mother and daughter—all must have drawn hearty
laughter from the members of the Court or from a popular audience. And in *The Play of India* too, the farcical elements are
uppermost. At the beginning, a woman is hypocritically lamenting
the departure of her husband for the Far East. When the ship is
well on its way, a Castilian comes to make love to the wife. On his
departure, another man arrives for the same purpose, and when
the first lover returns, the woman can only explain to her second
lover that the first is her "brother." Then to the consternation of

all, the maid reports that the husband's ship has unexpectedly returned to port, just as the wife is declaring that she will sing and spin, "certain of never seeing him again." The play ends with the arrival home of the husband (the lovers having escaped by the skin of their teeth), and the wife's maintaining to him that she has been most faithful, and heart-broken, during his absence!

III   The Play of the Fairies

The Play of the Fairies (*Auto das Fadas*), whose text may be found in *Obras completas*, V, 177–217, has been classified by Keates (p. 126), along with the later *Farce of the Gypsy Women* (*Farsa das Ciganas*) as simply "Court games," for their playful use of audience participation. *The Play of the Fairies*, in Portuguese and Spanish, is generally considered to have been performed in 1511, perhaps at Carnival time at the palace in Lisbon, in the presence of King Manuel, Queen Maria, Prince João, and Princesses Isabel and Beatriz, and the ladies and gentlemen of the Court (see Bell, *Four Plays*, p. xix). Thinking of the preceding simple *Play of Faith*, of the Salamancan Tradition, Bell states that *The Fairies* "further shows the expansion, perhaps we may say the warping of [Gil Vicente's] natural genius, for although we may rejoice in the presentation of the witch Genebra Pereira, the play soon turns aside to satirical allusions to courtiers, while the Devil gabbles in picardese. Peasant's *beirão* with a few scraps of biblical Latin had hitherto been Vicente's only theatrical resource as regards language."

The picturesque witch mentioned above salutes the members of the Royal Family, and wishes them well for years to come. Through her necromancy, she evokes the picardese-speaking devils, and two friars from Hell, who had been great lovers of women while on Earth. One friar says that he sang *Te Deum laudamus* with his eyes on Cupid, and before the audience's eyes he preaches a sermon (based on Virgil's Tenth Eclogue) on "Amor vincit omnia." Then three lyrical fairies cast spells, for good, over the members of the Royal Family and have them draw slips of paper for their fortunes. At this juncture, young Prince João, then nine years old, reads his father's fortune for him. "These verses on these little pieces of paper," writes Keates (pp. 126–127), "have no more value than the mottoes and riddles of

Resende's game" (as described in the *Cancioneiro* of 1516). In this game, on each card, for twenty-four men and twenty-four women, was written a fortune: twelve good ones and twelve bad ones. Each person drew his lot and read it aloud, and there was much merrymaking. "We need look no further for the inspiration and stage directions of Vicente's *Auto das Fadas*," concludes Keates very rightly (p. 24).

IV   The Farce of the Gypsy Women

The Farce of the Gypsy Women (*Farsa das Ciganas*), whose text may be found in *Obras completas*, V, 319–329, has been dated quite accurately by Braamcamp Freire as "1525." Simply to show that Gil Vicente continued his playful spirit throughout his career, *The Gypsy Women* can quite well be discussed here, out of its chronology. This little play, in Portuguese and Spanish, of only 222 lines, in eight and twelve syllable verse, has really no plot and pays no attention to characterization. In a manner similar to that employed in *The Play of the Fairies*, gypsy women tell the fortunes of the ladies of the audience while the gypsy men try to trade horses with the gentlemen. There is much singing and dancing, amid the comical gypsy language which is characterized by the lisping of the "s" and the "z" and the changing of every "o" into "u" (see Teyssier, pp. 254–264). The lisping of the sibilants was carried forward as "gypsy language" even into the Spanish *comedia* of the seventeenth century. This "court game," which like *The Play of the Fairies*, belongs to "farce" in a wide interpretation of the word, contains a slight satirical note: one of the gypsy girls remarks that she has never seen so many honorable people who give so little reward!

V   The Courts of Jupiter

In the matter of Court entertainment, which was, of course, Gil Vicente's purpose throughout his dramatic career, one very special evening comes vividly to mind. In the celebrations to wish Godspeed to Princess Beatriz who was leaving Lisbon, in August, 1521, to marry the Duke of Savoy, the height of Gil Vicente's comic talent was brought into play to provide a lively party. The drama he wrote and produced for the occasion was *The Courts of Jupiter* (*Cortes de Jupiter*), whose text may be found in *Obras completas,* IV, 225–260. In this play, in Portuguese and Spanish, Providence orders Jupiter, the king of the elements, to hold Court and to put into propitious order the planets and stars for the Princess' voyage to the distant parts. Mars, who will accompany and protect the retinue of eighteen ships, praises the Portuguese accomplishments in Africa and in the Far East, and generally pays homage to the Portuguese Royal Family. The royal princess is showered with gifts, and the play ends in much singing and dancing, as is to be expected. This is the only evening performance of Gil Vicente's for which we have a contemporary description (by Garcia de Resende), and special attention will be paid to it in a later chapter on "Gil Vicente the Impresario."

VI   The Triumph of Winter

In *The Triumph of Winter* (*Triunfo do Inverno*), a play reminiscent of the earlier *Play of the Four Seasons,* Gil Vicente celebrated the birth of Princess Isabel on April 28, 1529. Within this play's allegory (the text, in Portuguese and Spanish, is to be found in *Obras completas,* IV, 261–330) there are many elements of farce, and it is not out of order to include it in this all-embracing chapter on the comic *genre;* and in this particular reference to Court festivities, it is not out of place (although it is chronologically much later) to relate it to *The Courts of Jupiter,* for it had a very similar *raison d'être.*

Amid much of the customary lyricism, singing, and dancing, two shepherds complain about the harsh "triumphs" of Winter, while Winter, in the form of an old woman, is seeking a young husband (May). Further triumphs of Winter are revealed as sailors discuss a violent storm at sea. The first division of the play ends with Winter's being put to rout at the arrival of Spring. The play then enters its second division, which the author calls "The Triumph of Spring"; and amid other events, a quarrelsome discussion between a husband and a wife adds a farcical, realistic touch. Finally, Spring wonders what presents can be offered to the Royal Family to celebrate the birth of the princess, and it is decided that a fine gift would be the beautiful gardens of Sintra. Then four young men and four young women dancing and singing bring this Court entertainment to a conclusion. Noteworthy, as has been mentioned, are the play's many fine lyrics, often sung to a dance accompaniment; and an especially interesting one is where three sirens sing a beautiful ballad on the glories of Portugal, from the time of the first King Afonso Henriques down to the reign of João III. As Bell puts it (*Four Plays,* p. xxix), "The author introduced the play in a long lament in verse over the forgotten jollity of earlier times and then to show that his own hand had lost none of its cunning, he gave his audience a feast of lyrical passages in the Triumphs of Winter and Spring."

VII   The Play of the Doctors

But back to earlier farce! *The Play of the Doctors* (*Auto dos Físicos*), probably of 1512, contains the same plethora of wit and a modicum of satire, as previously seen in the farces on the poverty-stricken squire and the faithless wife. This *Play of the Doctors,* whose text, in Portuguese and Spanish, may be found in *Obras completas,* VI, 97–129, has been carefully studied for references to physicians and medicine by several critics.[1] Marques Braga (*Obras completas,* VI, 97) has declared it to be a "capital document for the history of Portuguese medicine in the sixteenth century." However, the farcical elements within the play were no doubt the attraction for the audience of Gil Vicente's time as they still are for a twentieth-century audience. And the main point of humor arises at the expense of a backsliding servant of the Church: a priest who falls ill because his beloved will not reciprocate his feelings for her.

In addition to the doctors who come in, one by one, to examine the priest's urine, to take the patient's pulse, to appeal to astrology, to recite "medical Latin" (which was used by later dramatists, including Molière in France) . . . , a most interesting character is Brasia Dias (cf. Brigida Vaz, the procuress of *The Ship of Hell*), a kind of Celestina, who has all kinds of remedies for the ills of love. However, she and the physicians, with their very comical language and slapstick actions, are unable to cheer up the love-sick priest, and a confessor is called. This priest-confessor confesses that he has been in love for fifteen years, and since love is ordained by God, no shame nor blame need be attached. In fact, he goes out to the "garden of Love" to bring back a "salad," a poetic medley "prepared by Gil Vicente," which is sung by four singers to cheer up the priest. (This same song, by the way, is also used in part in the early *Who Has Bran?*, and in the very late *Play of Lusitania* and *The Pilgrimage of the Aggrieved.*) After considering the majority of other comedies and farces on doctors, from the times of Ancient Greece to the beginning of the seventeenth century, A. da Rocha Brito concludes that *"The Farce of the Doctors* comes out victorious, scarcely surpassed by Molière's plays." As a result of its well drawn characters, its farcical actions and language, its humanity, its reality and its authenticity, this Vicentine play does indeed shine among the others of the type in World Literature.

VIII   The Old Man of the Orchard

The Old Man of the Orchard (*Farsa do Velho da Horta*), which has been assigned to the same year, 1512 (and whose text, in Portuguese, may be found in *Obras completas*, V, 141–176), is once again a farcical satire on everyday life; in this case the presentation of the antics of a ridiculous old married man in love with a young girl whom he has seen in his orchard. A main character is again a "Celestina," the go-between Branca Gil, who accepts many rewards from the old fool before being arrested and whipped by the authorities. She is a very living creature, as is the old man himself, who is left in sadness when he learns that the young woman is inclined to a younger man. The ridiculous nature of the play and its slapstick comedy are augmented by the "old goat's" putting on airs of youthfulness, singing and dancing, to be taken down a peg right on the stage by his scolding wife.

João de Almeida Lucas, in his edition of the play (Lisbon, 1943), believes that Gil Vicente had the very serious purpose in these farces (such as *The Doctors* and *The Old Man of the Orchard*) of combatting "with the scalpel of ridicule" (following the Horatian idea of *Ridendo castigat mores*) the moral laxness into which the Portuguese Nation had fallen. Many peasants, Almeida Lucas reminds us, had left the fields to flock to Lisbon (a point vigorously driven home in the later *Farce of the Carriers*); the dockside was swarming with adventurers and profiteers; life in general was one of pomp and show and luxury, and the phobia against work was rampant. Pleasure was the chief end of man, and his chief ambition was to rise higher and higher, and to enter, if possible, the Court of the King. Gil Vicente in the farces of this type, concludes Almeida Lucas, is fighting against sad reality: "Laxness of customs, immoderate ambition, vigorous reluctance for honest work."

IX The Play of the Widower

The Old Man of the Orchard may have been the last farce or comedy which Gil Vicente wrote for some nine or ten years (he was sufficiently well occupied with plays of other types, and particularly with the famous *Ships* and his *Soul's Journey*) if Charlotte Stern's argument for ca. 1521 is correct for *The Play of the Widower* (*Comédia do Viúvo*).[2] In this play, in Spanish (the text is to be found in *Obras completas*, III, 85–128), we have what seems to be a wider concept of comedy, and while it is still a very primitive piece, it is important to notice the "*Viudo*'s function in the gestation of Vicente's dramaturgy, particularly the *comedia*, a problem of serious concern to students of the Old Portuguese and Spanish theatres," as Mrs. Stern has put it. T. P. Waldron, in discussing the plays of chivalry by Gil Vicente,[3] found *The Play of the Widower* to be a primitive sketch of *Dom Duardos* (1522), and Zamora Vicente agrees that it is "a clear antecedent" of that chivalric play; for in both, among other details, a prince comes courting in disguise. I. S. Révah's contrary theory,[4] which is untenable, that *Dom Duardos* preceded and influenced *The Play of the Widower*, reminds one however of Fredson Bowers' wise statement regarding which form of a work precedes another in that "critical interpretation of evidence is at best inferential, and the logic of the argument is frequently reversible."[5] But in this case the probable date of the plays, 1521 for *The Play of the Widower* and 1522 for *Dom Duardos*, supports the Waldron-Zamora Vicente conclusions.

The first almost four hundred lines (of a total of 1506) of *The Play of the Widower* have very little to do with the main plot, and are devoted to the widower's references to the fine characteristics of his deceased wife and to the reactions to his great loss. This lament of the widower is a vivid echo, made very personal, of the frequently-mentioned *Couplets on the Death of His Father* (*Coplas por la muerte de su padre*) by the late fifteenth-century Spaniard Jorge Manrique, and contains, as Mrs. Stern states a "tone of acute despair . . . in sharp contrast to the calm resignation of Rodrigo Manrique in the face of death and the son's sadness but full acceptance of it." The widower's deceased wife was the sharer of her husband's sentiments and ideas—his "alter ego" —and indeed a perfect spouse, honoring and obeying her husband. In this, as Thomas R. Hart has said (*Obras dramáticas castellanas*, p. xxxvii), Gil Vicente is again reflecting his knowledge of Fray Ambrosio Montesino's *Epístolas y evangelios para todo el año:* "But you well ask: how must the woman show love for her husband? I answer, firstly, that she must honor her husband. . . . Secondly, she must obey her husband in all things, as St. Peter declares: 'Let women be obedient unto their husbands.'"

A friar urges the widower not to grieve (an act of rebellion against God), but to give thanks that the wife lived and died in a Christian manner. Then a crony, like other disgruntled husbands in Gil Vicente's plays, e.g., in *The Play of the Fair* (*Auto da Feira*), enters to express his envy at the neighbor's "good fortune." This crony, disillusioned concerning his state of blessedness, laments that his wife is still alive! This is clearly a farcical element, and within the tradition of medieval misogyny.[6]

It is worth while remembering that Gil Vicente's first wife, Branca Bezerra, died somewhere in the period 1512–14; and it is interesting to note that the two daughters in *The Play of the Widower*, Paula and Melícia, bear the names of Gil Vicente's elder daughter and of his second wife, respectively. These two lively girls are the mainspring of the action of the play proper, for a young prince disguised as a rustic and using rustic Spanish, falls in love with both of them! If we analyse this Dom Rosvel's character carefully—and his "protestations of love are a repetition of all the hackneyed courtly love clichés of the time" (Stern, p. 361)—we conclude that he is probably in love with love itself, and not with any person. Throwing aside his disguise, and revealing himself to be of the noble rank that he is, he appeals (making use of audience participation in the action) to Prince João, asking him which daughter he should marry. The Prince decides, logically, that it should be Paula, the elder; and fortunately for Melícia, Rosvel's brother, Dom Gilberto, through a *Deus ex machina* action arrives to pair off with the second daughter. The girls dress up in wedding finery, four singers sing enchantingly, and a priest marries the two couples. And here it might be interjected that this is a dénouement which will be used very frequently in the seven-teenth-century Spanish *comedia,* and which symbolizes, in the opinion of Alexander A. Parker, "the stability of the social order under the sanction of divine law." [7]

In this second part of *The Play of the Widower,* we are indeed in the realm of a broader comedy, or of a "romantic" play, rather than in farce itself in the strictest sense. Zamora Vicente finds in this play a technique of postponement of the main action for the sake of contrast and suspense, when, for example, the widower's crony comes upon the stage. This technique will be found once again in the Camilote-Maimonda episode of *Dom Duardos,* as it was found in the "Mofina Mendes" intervention in the *Auto da Mofina Mendes.* Zamora Vicente finds great merit in this method of conducting the action—and it is true that Dom Rosvel does finally appear dramatically to introduce the action proper, with promise of future movement and tension—but Charlotte Stern objects, however, that the effectiveness of the technique of delay, for suspense, can be seriously questioned, "since what is to be the main plot hasn't even been suggested." *The Play of the Widower* is, it must be confessed, a play which has many shortcomings dra-matically and Zamora Vicente in his enthusiasm to present a Spanish play by Gil Vicente in the best of lights overrated the piece, not putting it in its proper perspective in the evolution of dramatic techniques.

The greatest influence upon Gil Vicente for *The Play of the Widower*—and this may explain its being in Spanish—was Torres Naharro's *Comedia Aquilana,* to whose plot it bears much similar-ity. Torres Naharro's Collected Works, with a prologue on dra-matic theory, had been published in Naples in 1517, and by the time of the composition of the *Comédia do Viúvo,* those works had certainly reached the library of the Portuguese Court. "Is it not conceivable," asks Mrs. Stern rightly, "that in the *Viudo,* Vi-cente is applying his imperfect understanding of the Naharresque formula 'comedia no es otra cosa que un artificio . . . de notables y *finalmente alegres acontecimientos*' ['Comedy is nothing else than an artifice . . . of notable and *finally happy events*'] which the playwright himself later paraphrases in his *Comédia sôbre a Divisa da Cidade de Coimbra* [*Play on the Coat of Arms of the City of Coimbra*]? Certainly the play begins on a funereal note and ends as a festive wedding play with the characteristic wedding songs. Could it indeed be a transitional work, combining the static, monologue-type play or farce of the Middle Ages (first 388 lines) with the livelier, structurally more complex, *comedia a fantasía* of Torres Naharro (lines 389–1056) . . . ?" Mrs. Stern's plausible and thoughtful arguments do succeed in placing *The Play of the Widower* in a period of "transition," after Gil Vicente's initial attempt at farce (1508–1512), an initial continuation of the Salamancan Tradition (1513–1516), and the fine moralities (1516–1519) already studied.

X   The Play of Rubena

The Play of Rubena (*Comédia de Rubena*) (the text, in Portuguese and Spanish, is to be found in *Obras completas*, III, 3–83), belongs to the year 1521, for in November, 1520, Gil Vicente had been sent from Evora to Lisbon to prepare for the arrival of King Manuel and his Queen Leanor; and this play, and others, formed part of the subsequent festivities.

First of all, a licentiate, in a prologue, gives a résumé of the plot to the audience (in that type of prologue which came from Latin and Italian literatures and became widespread in the Peninsula through the influence of Torres Naharro after the publication of his Collected Works in 1517). The plot in brief is that in Castile an abbot had a daughter Rubena, who was made pregnant by a priest. The first scene of the play begins with Rubena's lamentations. A mid-wife is called; she in turn calls a witch, who in turn calls four devils. They carry Rubena off for the birth of the child.

The licentiate relates that a child has been born, and the audience sees the infant daughter Cismena in her cradle. Amid many lullabies, delightfully sung, two fairies arrive to cast good spells upon her, while predicting unavoidable troubles. The licentiate, to fill in the passing of time, relates that Cismena has become a shepherdess, at the age of five, and the audience sees her guarding goats, and held in contempt by the other shepherds and shepherdesses because she is a bastard. To protect her, her fairy godmother transports her to Crete to live in the house of a rich lady.

In the third scene, Cismena, now fifteen, has inherited the vast fortune of her protectress; and she is visited by a go-between (another Celestina), who is trying to overcome Cismena's inclination to renounce the world and become a nun. Amid the playing of musical instruments, the needlewomen sing the beautiful "The falcon who dares / with heron to fight," ("Halcón que se atreve / con garza guerrera"), which will be especially mentioned in a later chapter on Gil Vicente's songs. Cismena rejects many suitors, including a certain Felicio, who has as his page a disguised prince of Syria. Felicio, in despair, goes to the desert where he pines away for love of Cismena, and it is the "page's" sad duty to bring the news to the beautiful heiress. In due time, revealing himself to her as the prince he is (cf. *The Play of the Widower* and *Dom Duardos*), he is accepted by Cismena because "this love is true love."

It can be clearly seen that we are concerned here with one of Gil Vicente's fantastic comedies, of great lyricism and pageantry, very well suited to the royal festivities which occasioned it. In addition to the song mentioned above, and others which will be discussed in the later chapter on "songs," an "echo song," an artistic verse dialogue between Felicio and the goddess Echo, should be mentioned here, for it seems to point to a Salamancan play which Gil Vicente must have been reading at the time: Juan del Encina's *Eclogue of Plácida and Victoriano* (*Egloga de Plácida y Victoriano*), which has a similar echo song.

Judicious words by A. F. G. Bell (*Gil Vicente*, pp. 12–13) relate the play directly to John Gower and indirectly to Shakespeare: "The *Comédia de Rubena* is especially interesting because it is derived from the same source as *Pericles, Prince of Tyre*, and presents us in the person of Cismena with a Portuguese Marina, the common inspirer being John Gower in his *Confessio Amantis*, early translated into Portuguese and Spanish. Undoubtedly, Vicente's play owes more to this source than to Encina's *Plácida y Victoriano*, . . . from which it derived its echo-scene. *Plácida y Victoriano* is really the story of Pyramus and Thisbe (told in detail in Diego de San Pedro's *Sermón*) with a happy ending; the *Comédia de Rubena* is the story of a girl brought up far from her parents in a foreign land."

Upon *The Play of Rubena* fell perhaps more severely than in the case of any other Vicentine play the heavy hand of theological censorship. Prohibited entirely in the *Index Expurgatorio* of 1624, it had suffered deletions on several previous occasions. There is much anticlericalism within the play, it is true, for it is related boldly that Rubena is the daughter of an abbot, and has been made pregnant by a priest. In other words, Cismena's grandfather and father were both clerics. When a cradle is required for the baby, the witch sends the devils to the homes of friars or priests, because they all have babies! These references could be called Erasmian echoes in Gil Vicente,[8] but once more, as happens so frequently in Gil Vicente's works, they seem to be reflections of the common current of anticlericalism rampant throughout Europe. This anticlericalism, no doubt laughed at even by the clerics in the audience, was used by Gil Vicente as a criticism of morals, but very strongly no doubt for farcical purposes too. *The Play of Rubena* is a type of play apart from farce proper as such, but farcical elements are in it as we continue on our way through this evolution toward fuller-fledged and broader comedies of the chivalresque type (1522–1523), which will be discussed in a separate chapter.

Leaving aside for a moment then those important and extremely interesting chivalric comedies or tragicomedies (*Dom Duardos* and *Amadis de Gaula*, 1522–1523), we find that farce becomes uppermost once again in several plays of the mid-twenties. *The Farce of Inês Pereira*, the previously-discussed *Farce of the Gypsy Women*, *The Farce of the Judge of Beira*, and *The Farce of the Carriers* are important contributions to the jocular *genre*, and must have occasioned many a laugh through their comic scenes and many a tinge of conscience through their biting satire, when they were put on at Court.

XI   The Farce of Inês Pereira

The Farce of Inês Pereira (*Farsa de Inês Pereira*), whose text in Portuguese is to be found in *Obras completas*, V, 219–271, has been properly assigned in the *Copilação* to the year of 1523, with its first performance before João III in the Monastery of the Knights of Christ in Tomar. It, like the *Auto da Barca do Inferno*, is extant in a separate printed version of about the mid-sixteenth century, preserved in the Biblioteca Nacional, Madrid. I. S. Révah has used this copy, collating it with the *Copilação* version, to produce a useful edition of the play.[9]

The rubric of the *Copilação* declares that *Inês Pereira* grew out of a theme given to Gil Vicente to use for a drama: "I prefer a donkey which will carry me to a horse which will throw me" ("Mais quero asno que me leve, que cavalo que me derrube"), and from this the dramatist produced one of his best plays. In it, the heroine, tired of household tasks, rejects the "solid" son of a well-to-do neighbor-farmer, and chooses a squire who has all of the "showy" characteristics of his higher position in society. When after the wedding, her husband shows tyrannical unkindness and has her carefully locked up at home when he leaves for war, she can only sing philosophically: "The one who has good things, and chooses the bad, / Through whatever evil comes along, let her not be sad" ("Quem bem tem e mal escolhe, / por mal que lhe venha não se anoje"). A short while afterwards, it is Inês' good fortune to learn that her husband has perished in the wars; and in due time she accepts her former suitor Pero Marques. He will be the dull, solid donkey who will provide for her and put up with her whims, now that she is rid of the spirited "horse" which turned out to be a bad match.

Much comment has been published on *The Farce of Inês Pereira*, especially in the general books on Gil Vicente, and the general agreement is that the play is one of Vicente's best. The critics point to the superior unification of scenes, with a unity of action so frequently disregarded in the Vicentine theater, a greater amount of action, in a theater which is often slow moving or has no action at all, and a very fine presentation of character, which stands above many of the other attempts. Inês herself, her two husbands, her mother, a crony Leanor Vaz, and not at all the least the two marriage brokers, all are very attractive and living persons. Celso Láfer has given due attention to the study of the two Jews to whom Inês has recourse for a "better" match, and Láfer points out that the treatment of them is humorous and farcical, but always sympathetic. They speak in their ridiculous "Portuguese," they make compliments, they joke; and their candidate for Inês' hand is accepted by her. Their successful matchmaking thus leads up to the wedding and the wedding celebration which takes place on the stage, with singing and dancing, and much merriment—a marriage, which, it is true, was not the final one, for a second one came later, more to Inês' liking and convenience.

XII   The Farce of the Judge of Beira

Joaquim Leitão, in his study of women in Gil Vicente's plays,[10] has devoted several pages to the analysis of the heroine, Inês Pereira, who will be met once again (though off stage) in the later *Farce of the Judge of Beira* (*Farsa do Juiz da Beira*), of the year 1525 (the text is to be found in *Obras completas,* V, 273–317). The judge is the audience's old friend, Pero Marques, Inês' second husband, and he is able to relate that "My wife, Inês Pereira, / (May God bless her) knows how to read, / And knows all that I have need of / For me to properly carry out my profession" ("Minha hóspeda Inês Pereira / (Deos a benza!) sabe ler, / E quanto me faz mister / Para eu ir pela carreira").

In this play, in Portuguese and Spanish, which was performed before João III in Almeirim, Pero Marques tells the audience that he has now become a judge in Beira, his home province. To demonstrate his abilities, he has been called to Court to judge a series of cases, one after the other, in the presence of the King. First in comes Ana Dias, a real "Celestina," similar to other Vicentine go-betweens: Branca Gil of *The Old Man of the Orchard,* Brigida Vaz of *The Ship of Hell,* and Genebra Pereira of *The Play of the Fairies.* Ana's complaint is that her daughter has been raped in a wheat-field. Let the plaintiff and the accused be brought to court when the wheat is cut, decides the judge, in the first of his curious decisions.

Other unusual and unsatisfactory judgments are handed down when a new Christian (a converted Jew) complains that Ana Dias has brought about the dishonor of his daughter; when a squire complains that Ana Dias promised to obtain for him the favors of a Moorish slave and took his money without producing results; and when the same squire complains that his servant has taken clothing, with the servant putting in a counter-claim that he has not been paid for his services. The most comical case is one in which four queer brothers are quarrelling over their inheritance: one donkey. In court, one brother dances, one sleeps and snores, one fences, and one sings of love. The judge's decision is that the donkey should be summoned to a future court session. Meanwhile the judge tells them to go on with their dancing, sleeping, fencing, and singing, for he is going off to dine! The little play ends as the whole cast sings: "Let us go and see the girls of Sintra, / For the best things are in the mountains" ("Vamos ver as Sintrãs, / senhores, à nossa terra, / que o melhor está na serra").

This farce, almost slapstick farce, is far from the broader "comedy" of *Inês Pereira* and *The Play of Rubena*. It can be interpreted, in addition to its rough entertainment value, in which it is outstanding, as serious and conscious satire on the judges of the time who were appointed without proper qualifications (after all, it is the wife, Inês Pereira, who knows how to read!). In his study of law in Gil Vicente's plays, Luiz da Cunha Gonçalves is able to make comparisons, of this play, in tone and spirit, with Aristophanes' *Wasps*, in which one of the litigants, a dog, accuses another one of having eaten a Sicilian cheese without having shared it with his comrades.[11] He is able to point out, also, that *The Judge of Beira* is a fine example of Gil Vicente's plays' being "excellent documents, not only of linguistic and literary evolution, but also of usages, customs, laws, traditions, indumentaria, social states, public morality, etc., etc." And the critic goes on to remind us that it was not only the miscellaneous "smaller" vices of the nation that Gil Vicente was censuring on so many occasions, but that on some occasions at least he was condemning the broader abuses also. In the last play, for example, *The Forest of Deceits* (Evora, 1536), Cupid, greatly desiring a certain princess, succeeds in persuading her father to sacrifice the daughter's future happiness. Luiz da Cunha Gonçalves interprets this rightly or wrongly, but very plausibly, as a reference to the marriage, in 1526, of Isabel, daughter of the deceased Manuel I, to the powerful Emperor Charles V of Spain, "without love" and "for convenience of state."

XIII   The Temple of Apollo

For this marriage, Gil Vicente wrote and produced before the Court, in January, 1526, *The Temple of Apollo* (*O Templo de Apolo*). (The text, in Portuguese and Spanish, is to be found in *Obras completas*, IV, 159–190.) This palace piece is lyrical praise of the Princess and of the Emperor, and a formal act of homage to them. Those who are devotees of the Emperor and of his Empress are permitted to enter Apollo's temple; and so in comes a series of allegorical figures (World, Victory, Omnipotence, Gentility, Fame, Knowledge, etc.) and each one states his or her devotion to the illustrious couple and promises favor and protection. There is a great deal of the usual delightful music and singing; and comedy is introduced in the person of a Portuguese peasant, dressed as a pilgrim, who sings and speaks in a very witty fashion. Of interest at the beginning of the play is the coming on stage of the author himself to praise beautiful women and to excuse himself for the imperfections of his performance.

XIV   The Festival Play

The Festival Play (*Auto da Festa*), which has been plausibly assigned to 1525 by Bell (*Four Plays,* xxv, xxviii), is the one play, generally accepted as authentic Gil Vicente, which was not published in the *Copilação.* (The text, in Portuguese and Spanish, however, is normally in Vicente's Complete Works, and is to be found in *Obras completas,* VI, 131–169.) As has been noted in the first chapter, the *Auto da Festa* can be helpfully used to reach the widely accepted birth date of ca. 1465 for Gil Vicente. This play, which refers to Gil Vicente by name as its author, seems to have been acted in a private house in Evora, rather than under the usual Court auspices.

At the beginning of this brief farcical, and to some extent allegorical, satire on the "state of the Nation," Truth addresses the owner of the house in which the performance is taking place (rather than the King), complaining that worldliness, lies, deceits, and lack of fear of God are rampant. "But since you, sir, love me, I have come to you." As Truth sits enthroned upon the stage, various humorous scenes are enacted: first of all, a peasant from Beira complains that he is being prosecuted by a Judge because he lay with the Judge's wife (and she enjoyed it!). (This could be a reference to the earlier *Inês Pereira,* which ended with suggestions of future infidelity on Inês' part, and to *The Judge of Beira,* whose judge was Inês' husband, it is to be recalled.) Then a fool enters singing and proposes marriage to Truth. Then an old woman and a page, who are about to be married, seek a Church dispensation because they are blood relatives (but by the time the dispensation arrives the page has escaped). Two gypsy women, reminiscent of *The Farce of the Gypsy Women* of the same year, tell fortunes for the audience. Finally shepherds and shepherdesses flock on to the stage to celebrate a wedding in song and dance, for after all the old woman does catch a man: a peasant who is standing nearby! The whole is all very light and entertaining, lyrical and farcical, with, nevertheless, an undertone of satire on conditions in the nation which are not as good as they should be.

XV   The Farce of the Carriers

The Farce of the Carriers (*Farsa dos Almocreves*) wrote Bell (*Four Plays*, Notes, p. 78), "is one of the most famous of those lively farces with which Gil Vicente for a quarter of a century delighted the Portuguese Court and which still hold the reader by their vividness and charm." This farce was presented in 1527, in Coimbra, where the Court had gone to escape a plague in Lisbon. (The text, in Portuguese, is found in *Obras completas*, V, 331–369; and the original text and an English verse translation are in Bell, *Four Plays*, pp. 37–53.)

The plot, in brief, as the rubric of the *Copilação* relates, is that "a nobleman, of small income, lived in great state, having his own chaplain, goldsmith, and other officials, whom he never paid." It is the complaints of the chaplain and the goldsmith which make up a great deal of the play, and these references to the master's poverty have given the play, at times, the title of "The Play of the Poor Nobleman." However, as Bell states, "the extremely natural presentation of the two carriers in the second part justifies the more popular name." The carriers' episode is unified into the whole, for the carriers deliver parcels to the nobleman, and receive the usual non-payment meted out to all of his creditors. These delightful carriers, with their sprightly singing and rustic conversation, are of a Peninsular breed mentioned by many writers of customs, including Washington Irving, more than a century ago.

The carriers in Gil Vicente's play are gay, light-hearted, and philosophical in the face of disappointment. They are a breath of fresh air blowing upon the comical, but tragic, situation in which the nobleman lives with all his false values. It was a time, we can recall, in those years of the mid-twenties, when Portugal was becoming disillusioned about her hopes for what the East would bring, and the nation was full of persons who were upsetting the status quo, through ambitions to be something different and "better." The page had left his humble post as a goatherd in the hills for an alluring but disappointing job in town; the chaplain, the goldsmith, and even the nobleman himself are willing to sell their souls to be in the center of things and to achieve luxury; ease, and idleness. "What a difference in the state of the nation since [Gil Vicente's] first farce, *Quem Tem Farelos?*, twenty years ago!" exclaims Bell. Only the carriers seem to have common sense and the knowledge that every man can be of service even in a humble calling.

It is worth while recalling that in this same year, 1527, Gil Vicente was extremely busy with the production of an unusual number of Court plays of a light nature, all of which can be dealt with at this point through stretching somewhat the definitions of "farce" and "comedy." Perhaps it was rivalry with the "Italianate" and "modern" poet, Sá de Miranda, who had just returned from Italy with the hendecasyllabic line and its many stanza forms, such as the sonnet, that drove Gil Vicente to write the "miscellaneous" *Ship of Love (Nao de Amores)*, *The Play on the Coat of Arms of the City of Coimbra (Comédia sôbre a Divisa da Cidade de Coimbra)*, and *The Pastoral Tragicomedy of the Estrêla Mountain Range (Tragicomédia Pastoril da Serra da Estrêla)*, as well as *The History of God*, already mentioned.

XVI   The Ship of Love *and* The Forge of Love

The Ship of Love (the text is to be found in *Obras completas*, IV, 57–93) was written especially for the entry of Queen Catherine (sister of the Emperor Charles V) into Lisbon (1527), as *The Forge of Love (Frágoa de Amor)* had been for her betrothal to João III in 1524 (the text appears in *Obras completas*, IV, 95–126). Both plays are sheer entertainment, and lyrical comedies in the broadest sense; and both, in Portuguese and Spanish, were written to praise this new queen from Castile. Both are "supernatural," with many allegorical and mythological figures in them, and contain a superabundance of the usual songs and dances. In both there is a good deal of colorful staging, which will be discussed in a later chapter.

Into the "forge of Love," which is supervised by Cupid, as is to be expected, there enter various members of humanity, to be refashioned to their taste. On to the "ship of Love" go a prince of Normandy, with Cupid and many others, all seeking "Good Fortune." Even in this Court merrymaking there is to be found one of the characteristics of Vicentine farce: the satirical note. In *The Forge of Love,* Justice, in the person of a deformed hunchback, wants to be refashioned before the new queen arrives. The anvil chorus works on him, and the process is slow and difficult; but finally they do succeed in straightening him out. In *The Ship of Love* there is farcical anticlericalism: a friar has gone mad through love, and he speaks and sings at length in his witty, but also foolish, fashion. The anticlericalism is even stronger in *The Forge of Love,* for here is met a dancing friar who hates sermons and mass, but likes wine, women, and song. He wants to be reformed in a lay state, for his opinion is that friars are without number on earth. Júlio Dantas[12] feels that Gil Vicente was hitting at a truth which was very apparent in the Nation: "Each day there were more friars; each day more monasteries were founded in Portugal, and as the monastic population unproductive and parasitical increased, the Nation lacked manpower for agriculture, and for navigation, colonization, and war. It is against this state of affairs that Gil Vicente, inspired by strong political, economic, and social reasons, protests through the mouth of the irreverent Franciscan Frei Rodrigo."

XVII   The Play on the Coat of Arms of the City of Coimbra

The Play on the Coat of Arms of the City of Coimbra (Comédia sôbre a Divisa da Cidade de Coimbra), whose text, in Portuguese and Spanish, is to be found in *Obras completas,* III, 129–167, was written to praise Coimbra and to entertain the Court while in residence in that city in 1527. Gil Vicente explains the presence, on the city's coat of arms, of the princess, the lion, the serpent, and a calyx *(fonte),* and he gives his own explanation of the origin of the city's name and the name of the river Mondego, on whose bank the city stands. This fabulous and humoristic account of heraldry and genealogy has caught the critics' fancy for its entertainment value, and for the fact that it may be a veiled attack on Vicente's rival in poetry and drama, Sá de Miranda. Sá de Miranda's father was reputed to be a canon of the Church, and a person of that parentage is referred to in Gil Vicente's play. It seems to have been clear to the audience that Vicente was speaking of his rival, for Sá de Miranda came forth with an unmistakable reply in his *Fable of the Mondego River* (*Fábula do Mondego*) in the following year.

XVIII   The Pastoral Tragicomedy of the
Estrêla Mountain Range

The Pastoral Tragicomedy of the Estrêla Mountain Range (*Tragicomédia Pastoril da Serra da Estrêla*) was also produced for the Court in residence in Coimbra. Princess Maria was born on October 15, 1527, and the play was written to celebrate the event. (The text, in Portuguese, is in *Obras completas,* IV, 191–224; and the text, with English verse translation, is to be found in Bell, *Four Plays,* pp. 55–71.)

A figure representing the Estrêla mountain range (of some 6500 feet, and the highest in Portugal, in which Gil Vicente may possibly have been born), enters on to the stage to express joy at the Princess' birth. Shepherds and shepherdesses also come on to the stage to compliment the Queen, in song and in spoken verse. They then enter into lyrical and comical discussions of their own love problems. A fool is present, contributing comic witticisms, and a hermit is there too to have the shepherds draw lots for the shepherdesses. All pair off happily, and two professional players, Jorge and Lopo, arrive to help celebrate the joyful occasion, as the play ends in song and dance, to the accompaniment of organ music. "It is remarkable," writes Bell(*Four Plays,* p. 82) "that just at the time when Sá de Miranda had returned to Portugal with the new metres from Italy and was frankly contemptuous of Gil Vicente's rough mirth and rustic verse, Gil Vicente felt his position strong enough to present this lengthy play before the King and Court. . . ." "There is no action in the play," continues Bell very correctly, "and King Manuel would perhaps have yawned at these shepherds' quarrels, relieved not at all by the *parvo's* (fool's) wit or the hermit's grossness and only occasionally by a touch of lyric poetry; but perhaps these simple scenes were welcome to the growing artificiality of the Court." The interest of the play, Bell concludes, "lies in the customs of the shepherds and their snatches of song and in the intimate knowledge of the Serra da Estrêla shown by the author."

XIX The Play of the Fair

The Play of the Fair (*Auto da Feira*), of 1528, in Portuguese, whose text is in *Obras completas,* I, 195–245, can be included in this grouping of farces and comedies because of its severe criticism of the clerics and even of Rome herself. (Not that that in itself is farcical or comical, but the treatment, while no doubt serious enough in its conception is "farcical" in its nature.) Set in an allegorical form, the play follows the *Dialogues of the Dead* by the Greek Lucian, and the *Dialogue of Mercury and Caron* (*Diálogo de Mercurio y Carón*), of 1528, by Alfonso de Valdés (which must have reached Gil Vicente), in presenting Mercury who criticizes the materialism of the time and the blacksliding servants of the Roman Catholic Church. Mercury sets up a fair, and Time opens his booth to sell the fear of God and other virtuous wares. The Devil sets up his tent also, and puts on sale, with greater success, deceits, hypocrisy, and other evil goods.

Rome enters, and, as it has been her custom, she turns to buy the goods of the Devil. Later on, fortunately, she turns repentantly to Time's booth, when Mercury berates her for absolving others' sins while living in sin herself. Peasants come in, amid comical chatter, and turn first to the material things on sale, but seeing Time's virtuous wares are filled with awe at the marvels before them. The play then comes to an end, lyrically and optimistically, with a group of young women and men from the mountains, who have come to the Fair to pay homage to the Blessed Virgin. Amid dancing, they sing in two choruses the beautiful "Holy Virgin, / white and fair" ("Branca estais colorada, / Virgem sagrada"), as they leave the stage.

This play is the usual Court entertainment, with much lyricism and playful frolic, plus the serious homage to the Virgin in the finale; but it is also one of the most violent criticisms of the Church entered into by Gil Vicente. Once again one is reminded of Erasmus' bitter denunciation of the Church of his and Gil Vicente's time, but once again one is reminded of Marcel Bataillon's considered conclusion: that there is at best, in the non-existent Erasmus-Gil Vicente relationship, "a vague affinity of spirit." It is an anticlericalism held in common by the two writers coming from the Middle Ages, and not a direct influence of one man on the other. "Gil Vicente," states Bataillon (p. 214), "was not a Christian humanist, but the mouthpiece of an anticlericalism rooted from time immemorial in the people. He did not need Luther nor Erasmus to make fun of the bulls, the jubilees, and all the graces and benefits in which Rome was trafficking." While Gil Vicente applauds the popular dream of the final triumph of the True Faith—as for example, in *The Exhortation to War,* where Hannibal promises that the Christians will, with the aid of God, gain possession of all of Africa—he continues throughout his career to be fully within the current of anticlericalism rampant throughout Europe.

"Of all the contradictions which religious life of the period presents," wrote Johan Huizinga,[13] "perhaps the most insoluble is that of an avowed contempt of the clergy, a contempt seen as an undercurrent throughout the Middle Ages, side by side with the very great respect shown for the sanctity of the sacerdotal office." Huizinga explains this contempt, indeed "hatred," as due to a primitive "aversion felt by the savage for the man who may not fight and must remain chaste." It was the "feudal pride of the knight" that they esteemed; it was the worldly cleric, the "incontinent monk" and "guzzling priest" for whom they had no respect. "Hatred is the right word to use in this context," concludes Huizinga, "for hatred it was, latent, but general and persistent. The people never wearied of hearing the vices of the clergy arraigned." Gil Vicente, the critic of the clerical shortcomings of his time, was assured of an attentive audience even at Court, and even within the Church itself. But it is not surprising, however, that several lines of *The Fair* were suppressed by ecclesiastical censorship in the second edition of the *Copilação,* when Queen Catherine's protection was no longer at hand.

XX   The Priest of Beira

The Priest of Beira (O Clérigo da Beira), written "between September 1529 and February 1530" (Bell, *Four Plays,* p. xxix), returns to pure farce, of a slapstick nature. In this play, in Portuguese, whose text is found in *Obras completas,* VI, 1–45, two Palace servants trick a peasant and steal his hare and capons. The peasant then complains to the priest, who, with his son, tries to solve the problem. During all of these foolishly-treated actions, one of the most amusing characters is a Negro who, in picturesque language, adds a great deal to the farce.

But the play then loses its unity (as has not been infrequent in Gil Vicente), for a new episode and theme is introduced when the peasant's old mistress comes on to the stage bringing Cecília da Beira, a girl possessed by a spirit of prophecy, Pedreanes. The spirit speaks through the mouth of Cecília to predict the future of many of the courtiers present in the audience. In this play, we have once again "audience participation," in a bi-partite production, almost in the realm of court games. The second part has given from time to time to the play the title of *The Play of Pedreanes* (*Comédia de Pedreanes*), but the satirical and slap-stick farce of the first part (dealing with the Priest of Beira) remains the most interesting section.

XXI The Play of Lusitania

The Play of Lusitania (*Auto da Lusitânia*), of 1532, likewise contains two parts. This play, in Portuguese and Spanish, whose text is in *Obras completas*, VI, 47–96, presents a realistic first part portraying the home of a Jewish tailor; and a fantastic second part wherein members of the converted Jewish colony go to witness a play being put on by Gil Vicente to honor a new Prince (the complete *Play of Lusitania* was written to celebrate the birth of an heir to the throne, Prince Manuel). The first part is a very good sketch of customs in which the tailor, his wife and children, and a courtier who is wooing the eldest daughter, are portrayed and their life is described in a very vivid manner. The second part is allegorical fantasy so frequently found in Gil Vicente, in which, in this case, Prince Portugal comes from Hungary and falls in love with Lusitania, the daughter of a nymph, Lisibea, and the Sun. With the intervention of a troupe of gods and goddesses, amid much singing and dancing, and after many delays and indecisions, Lusitania decides to accept Portugal, and the play ends on a festive note.

The unifying feature is the move from the tailor's home to the palace to see a Vicentine play. But this is only a slight unity and each of the parts might have been developed into a full-fledged play on its own. Indeed, in a sense, *The Play of Lusitania* as it stands is really two short plays, and it can only be concluded that

Gil Vicente, careless of the requisites of usual dramatic technique, was influenced above all by the necessities of "court entertainment" when he gave his audience this type of thing. Laurence Keates (p. 124) finds that a play such as *The Play of Lusitania* is "neither fish nor fowl." But the audience seemed to have liked this mixture of a realistic element and a fantastic interlude, otherwise Gil Vicente would not have prepared plays in this way. However, this strange method of "pairing" was not without precedent in literary tradition, for as Charlotte Stern has pointed out, the majority of Juan del Encina's plays, when presented in the palace of the Duke of Alba were performed in pairs,[14] and Gil Vicente may have been following the master once more and transferring these entertainment devices to the Court of Portugal. Whatever the motives for this procedure may have been, those who charge the Vicentine theater with a lack of unity of action have ample reason to do so.

XXII   The Pilgrimage of the Aggrieved

Both *The Pilgrimage of the Aggrieved* (*Romagem de Agravados*), acted at Evora in honor of the birth of Prince Felipe in May, 1533, and the last play, *The Forest of Deceits* (*Floresta de Enganos*), presented in the same city before the Court in 1536, contain farcical elements which justify their inclusion in a chapter on farce and comedy.

In the first named play (whose text, in Portuguese, is found in *Obras completas*, V, 1–53), a peasant is aggrieved, or aggravated and distressed, at being unable to get his stupid son into a church position "to live at ease." Two gentlemen are likewise aggrieved through experiences in love; two nuns are upset at having to follow the rules of their convent; and two shepherdesses are annoyed at marriages planned for them. But, says Frei Paço, the interlocutor of the play, these annoyances must simply be forgotten; and to so do, and to salute the Queen and her new-born son, the aggrieved cheer up and end the play in song and dance.

XXIII   The Forest of Deceits

In the second play (whose text, in Portuguese and Spanish, is in *Obras completas*, III, 169–219), the audience is presented, farcically, with a series of deceits or tricks. For example, a poor squire, disguised as a woman, deceives a merchant through the sale of a false bill of exchange, and a king's daughter deceives Cupid by accepting the hand of another; but in the end the play reaches its dénouement with the usual merrymaking.

In this "last play which Gil Vicente wrote in his days," as the rubric in the *Copilação* put it, and in the previously-mentioned *Pilgrimage of the Aggrieved* too, Court entertainment of the comical and farcical, and at times fantastic kind, is uppermost. These plays and the others of this chapter are all part of that "comic talent" of Gil Vicente's which "holds us by its variety, its occasional insight into character, its vivid presentment of contemporary types, its mediaeval delight in contrasts. . . ." (Bell, *Gil Vicente*, pp. 17–18). All of these plays are very entertaining, and they fulfilled their purpose before the Court, even though at times they may irritate us by their shortcomings when viewed through the twentieth century's critical eyes. Fortunately, at times they went beyond their initial purpose of diversion to leave us something lasting and more enduring in the realm of theater, for as Bell has put it, "Gil Vicente's comedy is not exclusively of an external and burlesque kind. . . . There is also a more subtle and delicate humour in some of his situations and characters." Two of the best comedies (or they may be called tragicomedies since they include unhappy events before ending satisfactorily) are the plays of chivalry, *Dom Duardos* and *Amadis de Gaula,* and they will be discussed together in the next chapter.

CHAPTER 6

The Plays of Chivalry

G IL VICENTE'S two plays of chivalry, *Dom Duardos* and *Amadis de Gaula,* are among his most complicated and highly developed dramatic efforts. They are both in Spanish, reflecting the language of their sources, and, as is usual in the Portuguese sixteenth-century dramatist, are examples of exquisite lyrical verse, with *Dom Duardos* being by far the more poetic.

Dom Duardos was probably written in 1522,[1] and if so, was destined for a Court reading, since theatrical performances had been suspended for a period of mourning after the death of King Manuel I in December, 1521. On the other hand, the year 1525 is also possible, since there was a new edition of the source-novel in Seville, in 1524, and since the play may have been performed in a Court garden for the betrothal of João III's sister, Isabel, to the Emperor Charles V. (It is possible that the first date is its date of composition, and that the play was revived for the later Court celebration.)

Amadis de Gaula is dated "Evora, 1533" in the 1562 *Copilação,* and this date has been accepted by T. P. Waldron in his edition of the play,[2] but Braamcamp Freire, in his *Vida e obras de Gil Vicente,* and I. S. Révah both favor a much earlier date, with 1523 being suggested. The main argument for dates close together for the two plays, 1522 and 1523 respectively (the *Copilação's* 1533 could have been a misprint for 1523) is that Gil Vicente's attention was being directed, in the early 1520's apparently, toward the two Spanish books of chivalry from which he produced these plays of a similar type. The dates 1522 and 1523, then, seem the most likely.

I Dom Duardos

Dom Duardos, whose text appears in *Obras completas,* III,
221–306, and in a good edition by Dámaso Alonso,[3] is Gil Vicente's longest play, of some 2,054 lines. The work dramatizes in-
cidents from the Spanish *Primaleón,* Book II, whose first edition
appeared in Salamanca in 1512. There is a simplification and re-
duction by the Portuguese dramatist of the novelistic chapters,
and a new aesthetic existence, not previously possessed, is
achieved. The long title of the Spanish novel gives a good indication of the plot: *"Palmerín de Oliva,* which treats of the valiant,
brave deeds of arms of Primaleón, son of the Emperor Palmerín,
and of his brother, Polendos; and of Don Duardos, Prince of England, and of other esteemed knights of the Court of the Emperor
Palmerín." Of this novel, Gil Vicente has dramatized parts of
Chapters LXXX–XCII, XCV, XCVIII–CXI, CXXV, CXXVII,
CCVIII and CCIX in his own inimitable way, from the time of
the challenge to a duel up to the dénouement which is based on
Chapter CCIX, wherein "Don Duardos asked permission of the
Emperor to depart for England, and took with him his bride,
who, on their arrival there, was most graciously received." [4] All of
this material was presumably well-known to the audience in Portugal, which must have been delighted to see episodes from a fa-
vorite novel dramatized before their eyes, or at least read to them
dramatically.

The story of Gil Vicente's *Dom Duardos* then is that of his successful wooing of Princess Flérida of Constantinople at her father's
Court. His main stratagem is to disguise himself as her gardener
and meet her frequently as she enjoys the beautiful surroundings,
accompanied by her ladies-in-waiting. There are, of course, as is
to be expected in these fantastic tales of knights and ladies, many
complications of plot. For example, right at the beginning of the
play, Dom Duardos makes his appearance in the Court garden
and asks permission of the Emperor to avenge the death of Pere-
quín, who had been killed in a duel with the Emperor's son Primaleón, in a quarrel over the Lady Gridonia. The duel is begun (the
action seems to take place on the stage), but the Emperor has his
daughter Flérida stop it, lest two such worthy knights should per-
ish. Another complication of plot, which is almost an extraneous

episode and which Dámaso Alonso considers to be out of all proportion in length and in bienséance, is the participation of the knight Camilote, who challenges to a duel any man who will not confess that his ugly Maimonda is the most beautiful creature in the world.[5] Later in the play, learning that Camilote has killed several knights who were defending Flérida's reputation for beauty, Dom Duardos goes out in arms and armor to make an end of Camilote.

The course of true love, for Dom Duardos and Flérida, does not run smoothly. Dom Duardos must spend a dark, moonless night in the palace garden, a magic love potion must be drunk by Flérida, Dom Duardos must reject the temptation to yield to a girl of lowly rank who is anxious to have him; but in the end all turns out well, and the play terminates in exquisite verse, as the loving couple leave by ship for England:

> It was in the month of April
> One day from the month of May,
> When the roses and the lilies
> Don their loveliest array,
> And the night so calm and tranquil
> As e'er heavens might display,
> When Flérida the fair Infanta
> Was to start upon her way. . . .
> (Bell, *Lyrics*, No. 41, p. 87)

> (En el mes era de Abril,
> de Mayo antes un día,
> cuando lirios y rosas
> muestran más su alegría,
> en la noche más serena
> que el cielo hacer podía,
> cuando la hermosa Infanta
> Flérida ya se partía. . . .)
> (*Obras completas*, III, 304–305)

"This beautiful ballad," wrote Bell (*Lyrics*, p. 124), "became so popular as almost to become a traditional *romance*, and was frequently reprinted. The romantic Almeida Garrett included a Portuguese translation of it in his nineteenth-century *Romanceiro* and Menéndez Pelayo called it an *incomparable romance*." The evocation of legitimate young love, in beautiful Springtime, with flowers in full bloom, in a most delightful night, is but one more rhythmic example of Gil Vicente, the dramatic lyricist.

II   Amadis de Gaula

Amadis de Gaula, whose text is to be found in *Obras completas,* IV, 3–56, is based on episodes from the novel of chivalry of the same name. The first known edition is the Montalvo version, printed in Spanish, in Zaragoza, in 1508. Since *Amadis* was also a very popular book in the Peninsula as a whole, it is very likely that it was well known to Gil Vicente and to his audience.

T. P. Waldron, in his previously mentioned edition of the play, has analysed the Vicentine version very carefully in relation to its source; and once again it is evident that Gil Vicente has skilfully chosen and developed his source materials. Gil Vicente has apparently invented the first scene of the play, in which Amadis reveals to his brothers that he is in love with the beautiful Oriana (in the novel that fact is a carefully kept secret). After this revelation and confession, Amadis departs to enter into great deeds, as knights were wont to do, to make him worthy of his lady-love. When these exploits are recounted in due time at the Court of King Lisuarte, as an epilogue to affairs of state, the king's daughter, Princess Oriana, while pretending indifference, hangs on to every word relating to Amadis. Later, she sends her hero a message, asking him to meet her in her garden (a detail which Vicente found, for example, in Part I, Chapter 14, of the novel).

The course of true love does not run smoothly for Amadis and Princess Oriana (as it did not for Dom Duardos and Princess Flérida); and Gil Vicente introduces a scene of misunderstanding and half-repentance, absent in the novel. Mabilia, Oriana's companion (and Amadis' cousin) tries from time to time to mend matters, rather unsuccessfully, and Gil Vicente's "shrewish heroine" (as Waldron calls her) is usually making her suitor very unhappy through her stubborn lack of understanding. Amadis' dwarf too, through sheer mischievousness, complicates matters by declaring to Oriana that Amadis loves a young attractive queen, Briolanja, who has been dispossessed of her kingdom Sobradisa by her wicked uncle Abiseos. Amadis has been simply attempting to restore the queen to her throne, and he does not have any amorous interest in her. But Princess Oriana, in her jealousy, sends a further message to Amadis, rejecting him forever. In the novel, the dwarf's story is believed without hesitation, and the break between the lovers is made without delay, but in the play, Gil Vicente, with much more psychological insight and perspicacity, has his heroine enter into a long soliloquy in which, amid vivid dramatic suspense, she enters into feelings of doubt, hope, and a wavering between the two, before sending hesitantly, the letter of rejection. Princess Oriana, later very sorry in both literary works, sends a second, conciliatory letter, which persuades Amadis to return to his beloved. In the novel, which allows of greater length and narrative detail (but which is inferior in psychological realism throughout), the second messenger—the Maid of Denmark, to be exact—sails around the European seas and wanders through many lands before finding Amadis' whereabouts.

Gil Vicente has picked up, as can be seen, one of the best episodes from the novel, to develop it in a concise way into an interesting and moving drama. The characters are well presented; indeed much better presented than they were in the novel, for human nature occupies a minor place in the romance of chivalry. The Amadis of the Vicente play is, it is true, a typical knight of the literature of chivalry, with a touch of the hero of a *cancioneiro* poem in him; but he is a knight who is also a human man in love. Oriana is very true to life, of psychological complexity and interest, especially in the above-mentioned monologue of doubt. Mabilia, the friend and confidante, becomes the Princess' inner voice of conscience, paralleled by Artada and Amandria, Flérida's attendants in *Dom Duardos*, where the presence of two companions weakens the effect.

Waldron insists that an ironic and satiric treatment of the hero and of the story is a prominent feature in *Amadis de Gaula*. However, this is not the case.[6] There is no parody, nor any "decidedly anti-heroic treatment," and such was never the dramatist's intention. The play, far from being "very largely a satirical work," is on the contrary "the straight dramatization of a well-known romantic episode from a chivalresque novel." In Gil Vicente's day, "Amadis de Gaula was the sixteenth-century chivalresque hero *par excellence*," and it was not until later that parody, irony, and satire would be heaped upon these stories of chivalry, which Gil Vicente's audience knew very well and accepted with approbation. "*Dom Duardos* is a genuine romantic comedy," wrote Waldron. *Amadis de Gaula* is a genuine one also, not a dubious one, as Waldron would insist in his introduction to his edition of the play. Hart shared Waldron's opinion of *Amadis de Gaula* as a parody (*Obras dramáticas castellanas*, p. xlviii), but it is an opinion which is untenable, as was pointed out in the above-mentioned review of Waldron's edition; and it is an opinion with which Bruce W. Wardropper does not agree either: "The *Tragicomedia de Amadis de Gaula*, according to Hart and Waldron, its most recent editors, parodies the chivalric novel from which it derives, and thus approximates the world of farce. This is a view I do not share." [7]

Thomas R. Hart, in addition to the edition of the play in the *Obras dramáticas castellanas* (Madrid, 1962), had devoted a thought-provoking article to *Dom Duardos* in his study of courtly love in the play. [8] "The play," wrote Hart, "is deeply indebted to the traditional presentation of courtly love, familiar to Vicente and to his readers from the *Cancioneiros* and the romances of chivalry, but the traditional materials are very freely reshaped to meet the demands set by the action. . . . In the *Tragicomedia de Don Duardos,* he gives new life to the time-worn conventions of courtly love, precisely by insisting that they *are* usually conventions and then going on to show that, in this special case, we are not concerned with conventions at all but with deeply felt emotions." In this "doubtless the best known of Vicente's Spanish plays, thanks to both its own excellence and to D. Dámaso Alonso's splendid edition," we find, insists Hart, the usual theme of love demanding sacrifice from the lover; but here it is very new in that the sacrifice must be made, not by the hero, but by the heroine, for Flérida is presented with a test which she must pass, "just the reverse of the traditional situation in which it is the lady who sets the tests and the lover who must triumph over them." It is Dom Duardos who demands that Flérida return his love, on his terms, and their marriage will take place—as no doubt it will—in England, not in her own Constantinople among her family and friends. It is she who must make the sacrifice, and it is in this that the old tradition of courtly love is reversed, and something new, even "revolutionary," if we interpret it in that way, is presented to us.

Elias L. Rivers in his study of *Dom Duardos'* unity,[9] takes as his point of departure Dámaso Alonso's criticism of the play's "little care in dramatic unity" ("lo poco ponderado de su trabazón dramática"). Rivers, thinking particularly, as Alonso did, of the long drawn out Camilote-Maimonda episode, admits the play's "disunity of plot," but insists on its "close-knit poetic unity, based on a single well orchestrated theme"; the *Leitmotif* being "that intense lyrical yearning which the garden symbolizes for both Dom Duardos and Flérida; everything else in the play [being] related as subordinate variations on the basic theme of love." The extensive Camilote-Maimonda portion, it is true, does produce a rude contrast, as Dámaso Alonso suggests (no doubt Gil Vicente, fond of contrasts, put it in intentionally—for entertainment value and for variety's sake, to hold the audience's interest, just as Cervantes introduced extraneous episodes in his *Don Quixote,* Part I). But nevertheless, the Camilote-Maimonda presentation is but one additional illustration of the "miraculous omnipotence of Love," and is therefore, as Rivers states, "clearly relevant" to the central theme of the play: love, against the background of the garden, which is, as Dámaso Alonso has put it, "a mute character, who is in the minds and in the hearts of all, who presides over the action." With supersensitivity to the psychology of human nature, Gil Vicente leads us forward throughout the unified central theme, against a unified background, by means of a skilful use of a medieval verse of broken foot ("versos de pie quebrado"—eight syllables, with a hemistich of four—so frequently employed by him). And in the finale of this "symphony of love" there breaks forth the delightful ballad in which "To the rhythm of pleasant oars, / The princess fell asleep / In the arms of Dom Duardos, / For well she belonged to him" ("Al son de sus dulces remos / La princesa se adormía / En brazos de Don Duardos, / Que bien le pertenecía"). "Perhaps no other sixteenth-century play in Spanish," concludes Rivers, "has the close-knit lyrical and thematic unity of *La tragicomedia de Don Duardos;* every scene is an integral part of this highly original poem on the varieties and vicissitudes of love."

Bruce W. Wardropper has studied both *Dom Duardos* and *Amadis de Gaula* in the above-mentioned article on their "metaphysical sense," from the point of view of "the complex of metaphors which give coherence to the poetic world." For *Dom Duardos,* two predominant images are analysed: one based on the word "rose" (*rosa*) and the other based on the word "cloth" (*paño*). Wardropper has found these words, and the imagery associated with them, repeated throughout this dramatic work. The epithet of the rose is applied, significantly, first to the ugly Maimonda by her lover Camilote; then to Flérida by Dom Duardos as he annihilates Camilote on her behalf, and as he later cultivates her roses in her garden; and when he finally promises her "more beautiful gardens" in England, which Wardropper interprets as human fulfillment as a married woman. "Cloth" is first the justice or injustice which the Emperor, Palmerín, metes out in his affairs of state; "cloth" or "clothing" is put on by Dom Duardos to work in Flérida's garden, and to disguise his princely person. Cloths, or rather draperies, from Granada, embroidered with human figures, hang in Flérida's apartment, and again are but "ghosts or shadows" (*sombras*) of the real, the essential. The identity of each person, with the significance of surrounding imagery, becomes of prime importance in this metaphysical analysis of the play. In his poetic subconscious, Gil Vicente may have had Wardropper's subtle interpretation in mind; but it is very doubtful that consciously for Gil Vicente "rose" and "cloth" were anything more than the very appropriate concepts of material things which needed repeated mention as this play progressed.

It has already been noted that Wardropper objected to the Waldron-Hart interpretation of *Amadis de Gaula* as a parody approaching the world of farce. The drama, on the contrary, insists Wardropper, is a serious presentation, imbued with the tragic images of "death," "the desert," "drowning," "the sea." Amadis in his despair at losing Oriana's love went out into a desert to become a hermit; in other words, he died to the world. Even his name was changed: he decided to become "Beltenebrós." On the Peña Pobre (Poor Rock) where he took up his abode, he was in a desert physically, and also in the desert of his broken heart. Oriana, in her jealousy, would drown herself physically, as she would drown her own passion and Amadis' too. In the Amadis story, the audience knew that as an infant Amadis had been rescued from the sea, but now, in the play, it is a question of the opposite: of being destroyed in the sea—in a sea of enmity and deceit. The dwarf's false message of faithlessness had raised in Oriana's mind the question of what is truth, and had inspired the best psychological portrayal in the play. "Identity" in *Dom Duardos;* "Truth" in *Amadis de Gaula;* "two of the greatest riddles of metaphysics," concludes Wardropper, are found in these two plays of chivalry.

The two plays, *Dom Duardos* and *Amadis de Gaula,* are similar in their genesis, being based on Gil Vicente's recent readings in Spanish chivalrous literature. *Dom Duardos* is the more poetic, with songs and supernatural effects; *Amadis de Gaula* is the more dramatic, lacking to some extent in the first play's super-abundant lyricism and its marvelous events. Love is frustrated, temporarily, in both—and they can both be called tragicomedies—, but in the two love triumphs to bring about a satisfactory, happy ending. Both of the plays are deeply involved in an interpretation of courtly love; and reach, if we wish to interpret them in that way (without being certain that it would have been Gil Vicente's own!) a meaning deeper than their outward trappings. Both of the plays are, indeed, among the best of Gil Vicente's works.

CHAPTER 7

The Miscellaneous Works

G IL VICENTE'S *Copilação* of 1562 contains, in addition to the plays, a few miscellaneous works: some poems and prose passages, which are arranged in a final section entitled "Verses and Small Things" ("Trovas e Cousas Miúdas"). Some of these writings are clearly connected with Gil Vicente's position at Court; others are less easily assigned to any particular event or occasion.

I *Have Mercy on Me, O God*

The first selection in this miscellaneous section is a paraphrase in verse, in Portuguese, of Psalm L: "Miserere mei, Deus, secundum magnam . . ." ("Have mercy on me, O God, according to Thy great mercy, and according to the multitude of Thy tender mercies blot out my iniquities"). (The text is to be found in *Obras completas,* VI, 171–178.) This is the most beautiful of the penitential psalms, and the only biblical text which Gil Vicente translated or paraphrased in its entirety. Juan del Encina, in his *Cancionero* (1496), had previously written a paraphrase of the same psalm, and Gil Vicente, in his version, may or may not have been working independently of his Salamancan "master." Certainly the form is similar to Juan del Encina's: *quintilhas* for each strophe, in eight-syllable lines, with two rhymes in each five-line stanza. Also, as Marcel Bataillon has pointed out,[1] Savonarola's meditation on the *Miserere,* written in prison, and the last message of the martyr, certainly influenced Gil Vicente's thought and presentation. The first forty lines of introduction are clearly from the "moving introduction by the Italian monk." And it is to be remembered that the Savonarola version ran through several Spanish translations in the sixteenth century: Alcalá de Henares, 1511, for example; with a possible Portuguese translation printed in Lisbon, 1532. In fact this last possibility has inspired some critics to believe that Gil Vicente may have written his paraphrase right after that date, in his last years, as death seemed to be coming upon him.

While the date and circumstances of Gil Vicente's version still remain in some doubt, Bataillon rightly insists that Vicente was at least *remembering* Savonarola as he wrote. In fact, six lines apparently missing in the 1562 Vicentine text can be supplied directly from Savonarola. For his whole composition Vicente may not have had Savonarola directly before his eyes, but much of the Portuguese dramatist's depth of understanding, sincerity, and religious fervor, in flowing lyrical verse, may be due, not only to the original Latin source and to his own theological interests and beliefs, but also to the noteworthy *Devotísima exposición sobre el psalmo de Miserere mei Deus,* by this fifteenth-century Italian theologian, which Gil Vicente certainly knew, at least in a Spanish translation.

While some of these miscellaneous works cannot be dated, an early "sermon," prepared at the instigation of the dowager Queen Leanor, was "preached" before King Manuel and his Court in Abrantes, in 1506. The occasion was the birth of Prince Luis. The language employed was Spanish.

II *The Sermon*

The first twenty-four lines of the *Sermão* are introductory: to excuse himself, says Gil Vicente, for passing beyond "the limits of his jurisdiction" (theater) into philosophical-theological reasoning, which was not part of his duties, or privileges, as a lay person. His asking pardon of his "detractors"—and that word is used in the fourth line of the poem—has inspired Carolina Michaëlis de Vasconcelos to believe that the theme of the sermon was imposed upon the dramatist by those who had thrown doubt upon his ability and originality[2] (and a similar tradition has grown up concerning *Inês Pereira*). The subject of the sermon proper is drawn from an inscription, the author tells us, seen by him written on the wall of a corridor or anteroom of the Abrantes Palace: "Non volo, volo, et deficior," and interpreted by him, in three parts, as "I do not want (to), I do want (to), and it is vain (to)." Commending himself to the Blessed Virgin, and admitting his ignorance and inabilities, he goes forward to illustrate the tripartite motto.

The first part of his preaching is based on "I do not want"—to explain the Trinity; to enter into a discussion of the words of St. Augustine and other Church Fathers; to enter into various theological and historical questions. "I do want," Gil Vicente insists, however, to tell you, the listeners, that through many signs it is evident that the world is drawing to an end. One sign is that justice, truth, faith, and fear of God have departed from the World; a second sign is that the World no longer recognizes right from wrong, in short, it does not know anything good. A third sign is that it does not see the certainty of its perdition; a fourth is that it grasps or steals everything that does not belong to it. In fifth place, there is no contentment, no gratitude; sixthly, the World accepts no divine assistance; seventhly, its hands and its feet are too cold to do anything right. The eighth sign of decadence is that it stammers and can say nothing properly. Finally, the ninth sign is that the World is gnashing its teeth, it is making grimaces of despair. In short, through all these signs, civilization is manifesting its impending doom.

The third, and concluding, portion of the sermon is very brief: what it is vain to do. "It is vain" to preach truth, to ask for virtue, to reprehend evil, to praise goodness (for it does not exist), to sow seed on sterile ground. . . . In short, concludes Gil Vicente, "this sermon is in vain." So, asking pardon of God for his temerity, and commending himself once more to the Virgin, and to her Son, he brings his sermon to a close.

In this preaching, there seems to be no connection with the occasion which was its *raison d'être*. In fact, it seems rather inappropriate in its tone and presentation for the celebration of the birth of the "Illustríssimo Iffante Dom Luis." Unless the explanation is that it was being preached while waiting for the Prince to be born, as the rubric may imply, and it was intended to make the Court reflect on the transitoriness of birth and life, and the certainty of death. How serious Gil Vicente intended his composition and presentation to be, or how seriously it was received, it is hard to say, but throughout it all joviality and wit are not lost from view. In it there are subtle little exercises of irony and satire. The repetition of "I do not want" and "I do want" are brought to a happy conclusion in the "It is vain." The references to holy things are sincere and devout (there is, for example, a paraphrase of the prayer *Ave Maria*); but the jibes at the Church on earth and its backsliding servants are frequent. The sermon could be characterized as clever comment on the state of the nation; a state hardly fitting to receive the new-born prince, if Gil Vicente's damning criticism is to be literally believed.

III   *To the Memory of Manuel I*

The above sermon was preached, or rather recited or read, before King Manuel. A good many years later, in his function as "poet laureate" of the realm, Gil Vicente would compose a poem "to the memory" of that great king, who died in December, 1521. This national lament (whose text is to be found in *Obras completas*, VI, 201–212) is in Portuguese, except for some lines in Spanish quoting the words of sorrow of the "foreign" widow, Dona Leanor, Manuel's third wife. It is very proper that she should break into her first-learned language in a moment of deep grief. The whole composition is a conventional one, but Gil Vicente's poetic gifts and dramatic sense make the literary effort a living vehicle for the mourning of the nation at large and of the members of King Manuel's Court in particular.

The introductory lines of the "In memoriam" make the reader feel that Gil Vicente has turned directly to the famous late-fifteenth century *Couplets* (previously mentioned), which Jorge Manrique, in Spain, had written on the occasion of the death of his noted warrior-father Rodrigo Manrique. Gil Vicente's reference to the vanity, deceit, and fleetingness of physical life on earth are highly reminiscent of Jorge Manrique's universal expression of grief, which has been so ably translated, in modern times, into English verse by Henry Wadsworth Longfellow. Princess Beatriz's brilliant departure for Savoy, it is to be recalled, had taken place only a few short months before (with the performance of *The Courts of Jupiter*, amid other festivities), and that height of worldly pomp and pageantry followed by this "disaster" is taken by Gil Vicente to be an example of the fickleness of Fortune and of things of the World. The fact that the King, "so healthy and so strong," had suddenly departed from the earth, as a result of a mortal fever, was a shock to all of Portugal.

The introduction to the "elegy" is followed by a ballad, which imitates the very common old ballad of lament: "There is weeping in Lisbon, / on this St. Lucy's day, / For the King Dom Manuel, the Good, / Who has departed on his way" ("Pranto fazem em Lisboa, / dia de Santa Luzia, / Por El-rei Dom Manuel, / Que se finou nesse dia"). Here we have the use of a conventional literary form to pour forth the grief of the Royal Family: the mournful words of Princess Isabel (later to marry the Emperor Charles V) are quoted, and also those of the widowed Queen Leanor, very properly in Spanish, as has been noted above. The Crown Prince, soon to be acclaimed João III, sighs amid "prudent tears." As in a flash-back to the immediately preceding scene, the King's pious death is described: he received the last rites of the Church, and "gave up his soul to Whom he owed it." In a coffin, then, they carried him from his Ribeira Palace (where he had seen so many of Gil Vicente's plays performed) amid torches, a few hours before dawn, to the resting place of Kings, the Belém Monastery of the Jerónimos, for which Gil Vicente had, under Manuel's auspices, labored long and skilfully to produce the Belém monstrance from the first gold tribute from the East. In that holy place, as they laid him to rest—Gil Vicente describes the scene very vividly as an eye witness—the grandees of Portugal addressed prayers to the Virgin Mary, commending Manuel's soul to Her. Some eleven short prayers, by eleven counts and dukes, were written down by Gil Vicente. That he may have been using his creative imagination to embroider them even (Garcia de Resende, also an eye witness, implies in his *Miscelânea* that Dom Manuel was not so sadly mourned), does not detract from this very good brief literary elegy that Gil Vicente has left to us among his Miscellaneous Works.

IV *For the Coronation of João III*

It was the duty of the Court poet-dramatist not only to lament the departed, but also almost simultaneously to celebrate the new Monarch as he ascended the throne about ten days later, on December 19, 1521 ("The King is dead; long live the King!").

This happier event occasioned another dramatic poem, in ballad form, not inferior to the preceding: "On the nineteenth of December, / Close it was to Christmas day, / In the fair city of Lisbon, / Very noble and always loyal, / There ascended to the throne as King / Of the Kingdom of Portugal / Prince Dom João III, / A Prince angelical" ("Dezanove de dezembro, / Perto era do Natal, / Na cidade de Lisboa / Mui nobre e sempre leal, / Foi levantado por Rei / Dos reinos de Portugal / O Príncipe Dom João, / Príncipe angelical"). (The text of the poem is in *Obras completas,* VI, 213–225.) Carolina Michaëlis de Vasconcelos has pointed out that the two poems, on the death of one monarch and the coronation of his successor, may be considered to be a single bipartite work, for the two of them do form a unified whole, closely connected in treatment and personal loyalties.[3]

In the second poem, on the coronation, the praise of the new King's qualities, as was the case in the first poem, is highly exaggerated, for Gil Vicente never forgot that he was the servant of his royal masters. Nevertheless, there is a sincerity and lack of subservience which does the poet credit. Once again we have a very vivid description, perhaps embroidered also by poetic enthusiasm, of an eye witness. Prince Luis, on the occasion of whose birth the sermon of 1506 had been "preached," was there with other members of the Royal Household; and he and his royal companions attended the new Sovereign as he rode forth to the Cathedral of São Domingos, where his uncle Afonso, the Cardinal-Prince, gave him his blessing and received his oath of dedication and service. Amid the proclamation of the new King, and the blowing of trumpets, the grandees moved forward for the "beija-mão" (the kissing of the hand) and the oath of loyalty to their new Sovereign and Liege Lord.

"I was there," continues Gil Vicente in verse, "but so far away that I couldn't hear their words." So Gil Vicente imagines what these nobles of the realm probably said: much flattery, mixed however with some good advice; the best of the latter being perhaps from the Conde Almirante that João III should be his own master, and not allow himself to be governed by others. This piece of advice was apparently not followed however, for the King came to be dominated entirely by his Spanish wife, Queen Catarina, who favored her fellow-countrymen to the detriment of the Portuguese. Complaint on this very point was presented to King João himself, half seriously and half humorously, in some later verses which are published at the end of the *Obras miúdas* in the *Copilação:* "To whom shall I present my complaints, / great Sire, / if not to you?" ("¿A quién contaré mis quejas, / gran Señor? / ¿A quién contaré mis quejas, / si a vos no?").

V *A Complaint*

These thirty-six lines, in Portuguese and Spanish, which are in *Obras completas,* VI, 257–259, are in the usual verse combination of eight and four syllables. Their subject matter, the rubric tells us, was inspired by an argument which Gil Vicente had with some Castilian carriers as he returned from Coimbra to Santarém. He felt that they had grossly overcharged him, because the Queen had ordered that Castilians should not be required to work for fixed wages, but "for the price which they wished to set." This Spanish queen of Portugal was not willing, like Ruth, to proclaim "Thy people shall be my people, and thy God my God" (Ruth I, 16). Indeed Gil Vicente's experience and historical comment portray her otherwise; and Gil Vicente does not hesitate, within his poem, to bring to the King's attention the fact that the Castilians took from him all he had, because they were enjoying the Queen's protection. His solution, in this particular case, would be to have restitution made through João III's Minister of the Treasury, Fernand'Alvares de Andrade, mentioned also in *The Pilgrimage of the Aggrieved,* and who was known for his generosity and promptness in payment. And, in passing, it might be said that Queen Catherine evidently did not hold this witty complaint against Gil Vicente, for it is to be recalled that it was she who, as a widow in the mid-century, encouraged and protected the publication of the Collected Works (1562).

VI *The Epistle-Dedication of the Copilação*

João III was the recipient of at least two other communications from Gil Vicente. One is an epistle-dedication to the *Copilação,* which indicates that the dramatist was at least planning, before his death, the collecting and editing of his complete works, which task was continued and brought to a conclusion, as is well known,

by his son Luis some fifteen years after his father passed from
the scene. This prologue, in Portuguese (*Obras completas*, I,
lxxix–lxxxi), is very brief, of about two pages in length. The vehicle used is prose. Speaking respectfully and humbly, the dramatist
asserts that his works cannot be compared with the elegant writings he has seen in print. Therefore he has felt very hesitant to
bring forth "the poverty of his wit"; but the King has encouraged
him to do so, and in his dilemma he has decided to proceed with
their preservation for posterity. The main reasons which have
swayed him to positive action are that, since many of the plays are
works of devotion, the printing of them will be not only in the
service of the King, but also in the service of God.

It is not surprising that the Court poet-dramatist should thus
express his appreciation to his patron for the many benefits received and the many still hoped for. The phraseology employed
seems flowery and exaggerated, when Gil Vicente speaks of the
King's "magnificence, kindness, most noble character, perfect zeal
for justice, wisdom, liberality, prudence, most Christian fortitude," etc., etc., all in one breath. But dedications of this kind
were traditionally embroidered in those centuries, and no unexpected or unusual characteristics are to be found in this one. The
prose is smooth and colorful, and, one might add, almost poetic.
The autobiographical elements are two: that Gil Vicente was
aware of the printed page around him (unfortunately he mentions none of the authors he knew), and that, in his "old age," he
had become personally involved in the compilation of his works,
to please and to serve His Majesty.

VII *A Letter for Tolerance*

The other communication which we must bear in mind—one
which is of considerable significance—is a "letter" (in Portuguese
prose) which Gil Vicente sent to João III, who was in Palmela, in
January, 1531. This letter, whose text is in *Obras completas*, VI,
251–255, reveals very clearly the dramatist's sympathy for humanity and his noble tolerance for and understanding of elements
within the nation, who were "foreign" in both religion and blood.
On January 26, 1531, an earthquake had shaken Portugal; and
according to this letter, which describes subsequent events, the

friars of Santarém, where Gil Vicente was staying, made two declarations: one, that the unusual, terrifying phenomenon was due to God's anger at the sins of the Nation (part of which, at least, was the tolerance of the presence of suspect "New Christians" or converted Jews); and second, that another earthquake, caused by the same reasons, would occur on February 25 of the same year. Gil Vicente's concluding remarks in his letter show that the alarmed populace of Santarém would have turned their alarm and terror against the converts, suspected of theological infidelity, had not Vicente risen up to refute the friars on the two points they had raised, in the Church of São Francisco.

Firstly, insisted Gil Vicente, as he relates it to the King in his letter, the earthquake was not due to the anger of God, as a warning and punishment for sins, but a very natural phenomenon in a Nature which is filled with contrasts. Some of these contrasts, according to Gil Vicente, are the beauty of Spring and the heat of Summer, the vigor of youth and the infirmity of old age, poverty and wealth, the rise and fall of Rome, the excellence and the destruction of Jerusalem. . . . An earthquake, therefore, can come not unexpected in the normal history of things. Secondly, to the fanatical and superstitious friars of Santarém, whose reaction was due more to "ignorance than to the grace of the Holy Spirit," he points out, or at least he writes to the King that he pointed out in his "sermon" in São Francisco's, that God has ordained that no one should be so bold as to interfere with the things that are to come nor to try to predict those things, nor even wish to know them, "because that belongs to the omnipotence and omniscience of the Father." Also, he reports that he told the friars, returning to the first point, that if there were many sins being committed in the Kingdom of Portugal, there was also much piety and many pious works being performed. Likewise, he told the friars, if there were some people in the nation who were still strangers to the True Faith, they should be lovingly encouraged to join in with the Christians wholly and sincerely, and not to be maligned and roughly misjudged to please the emotions of the easily roused rabble.

The result of his good sermon, Gil Vicente wrote to the King, indeed a sermon which he prepared and delivered as he himself was "near to death through illness," was that at the next day of preaching all of the preachers followed his example in tolerance and good will to all mankind!

VIII   *The* Verses to Felipe Guilhem

A small body of the Miscellaneous Works is made up of some very brief and inconsequential versifying. The *Verses to Felipe Guilhem (Trovas a Felipe Guilhem)*, whose text, in Spanish, are recorded in *Obras completas*, VI, 197–200, are some sixty-five lines addressed to a Castilian adventurer by that name, who arrived at the Portuguese Court in 1519, claiming to be an expert in all of the sciences of the day. He did construct, among other things, an astrolabe, and was granted a pension by the King. However, an expert in mathematics and astrology from the Algarve, where in the preceding century Henry the Navigator had founded his famous School of Navigation, one Simão Fernandes, revealed him to be an impostor. As Felipe Guilhem was escaping on horseback, he was arrested, and taken to prison. Gil Vicente addressed this short poem to him, ironically, "because he was a great poet." The tone of the composition is sarcastic, as Vicente speaks of Guilhem's prosperous fortune and then his fall. The catastrophe was due, Vicente insists, to the Castilian's having "sold false cloth" (reminiscent of an interpretation of poetic imagery in *Dom Duardos*). The *Verses to Felipe Guilhem* are of small literary value, and can be accepted only as comment on an event of the day, in rather witty verse.

IX   To Afonso Lopes Çapaio

Some Portuguese lines *To Afonso Lopes Çapaio (A Afonso Lopes Çapaio)*, found in *Obras completas*, VI, 245, were inspired by a poetic contest, held by an unidentified "new Christian" from Tomar (Braamcamp Freire, among others, declares his inability to make the identification). The contest was to elaborate, poetically, upon the jingle "Matou-me Moura e não mouro / E quem m'a lançada deu / Moura ella e mouro eu." (The play on words makes an English rendering difficult, but something like this will give the meaning: "I was killed by a Moorish girl, / Not by a Moor. / She was the one who gave me the lance thrust. / Now she remains a Moorish girl and I a Moor")—i.e., we are both captives of Love. Picking up this three-line starting point, Gil Vicente continues on for eight additional lines (see *Obras completas,* VI, 245), playing on the idea of a Moorish girl's wounding, through Love, a Christian, who was never so attacked before.

To the same Afonso Lopes Çapaio, Gil Vicente addressed some rather vulgar lines in verse, "as he lay ill from dysentery in Santarém" (*Obras completas,* VI, 246–247). The vulgarity arises from the description of disagreeable physical symptoms; and the rough earthiness presented here is far more indelicate than any such expression which arises, only occasionally, in the farces.

X   To the Conde do Vimioso

To the Conde do Vimioso, the dramatist addressed a few lines in Portuguese verse, commenting on a plague from which the country was suffering. Very interesting from a literary point of view, in the same communication (see *Obras completas,* VI, 248–250), is Gil Vicente's allusion to a "very fine" farce of his which he had before him: *A Caça dos Segredos* (*The Hunt for Secrets*). Aubrey F. G. Bell was inclined to believe that this was the play known to us as *The Play of Lusitania,* and if so, the verses to the Conde do Vimioso can be dated as 1532. This verse "letter," to an important man of the realm, concludes with the usual words of courtesy and respect; the author's whole preoccupation is to please the Count and to give expression to the affection he has for him. But, says Vicente, the more loyal the service, the less the pressing for reward. Therefore from him there has usually come but silence!

XI   Vasco Abul's Lawsuit

Outside of the *Copilação,* and in the *Cancioneiro Geral* (1516), edited by the courtier-poet and historian, Garcia de Resende, is one humble poetic contribution by Gil Vicente. This is a contribution of sixty-odd lines to "Vasco Abul's Lawsuit" ("Processo de Vasco Abul"), and a witty bit of versifying and participation in an evening gathering at Court when the Royal Household was amusing itself to while away the time. The burlesque "lawsuit" (or Court discussion in verse of one of the courtier's problems) arose from the fact that the courtier Vasco Abul had given, in jest, a gold chain to an attractive dancer, and the girl had refused to return it to him. The "judge of the case" is Anrique da Mota (mentioned before as a forerunner of Vicentine farce), and the dowager Queen Leanor is present too. After Vasco Abul presents his complaint, and several courtiers give their opinion in clever verse, Gil Vicente gives his opinion too: that it was a matter of love, the girl deserves her reward, and Vasco Abul has no cause for complaint. A more developed type of dramatized lawsuit appeared later in some of Gil Vicente's plays, it is to be recalled (such as *The Judge of Beira* and *The Pilgrimage of the Aggrieved*); and later dramatists such as Cervantes made good use of this type of thing in humorous interludes such as *The Judge of the Divorces* (*El juez de los divorcios*). It was not bad practice, then, for Gil Vicente to have been playfully versifying, in a dramatic way, with the Court poets of the *Cancioneiro Geral*.[4]

XII   Maria Parda's Lament

Last, but far from least, among Gil Vicente's Miscellaneous Works to be considered in this chapter, is *Maria Parda's Lament* (*Pranto de Maria Parda*), which appears in *Obras completas*, VI, 227–243.[5] This dramatic poem is certainly, as Luciana Stegagno Picchio has declared in her recent edition,[6] one of Gil Vicente's "most fascinating works." The date of composition is, as Maria says in the text itself, the year 1522. The problem is, in the 369-line poem in Portuguese, that wine is so dear and scarce that she is dying of thirst. Very vividly she names the streets where, in vain, she has sought to satisfy her desire, and very dramatically she enters into conversations with tavern keepers, who send her away, because they have nothing to serve her or because they are unwilling to extend credit to her.

Finally, in her despair, Maria Parda decides that she is going to die of "dryness," and so in this "sad era of twenty-two A. D.," she will make her last will and testament. This comical document occupies about 125 lines of the poem, and complements the buffoonery of the preceding lines. To Noah, who planted the vine, the heroine naturally commends her soul. Her body, she wills, is to be buried in a place where people are "always engaged in drinking." Her funeral mass is not to be a dry one.

This burlesque lament seems to have been modelled on some verses which have already been mentioned, *The Lament of the Priest* (*Pranto do Clérigo*), by Anrique da Mota (printed in the

Cancioneiro Geral). Here Anrique da Mota presents a cleric who is much upset by the loss of some very good wine. Gil Vicente's poem, too, may very well be, consciously or unconsciously, in a medieval tradition of such buffoonery. And its direct inspiration may very well have been the state of the Portuguese nation. King Manuel, it is to be recalled, died in December, 1521, and João III was proclaimed sovereign in the same month. The year 1522 was a very bad one, with famine and want throughout the land. Even bread, not to say wine, was unavailable to the many who flocked to Lisbon hoping for assistance. Nor could neighboring countries alleviate the plight of the Portuguese, for Spain had suffered a crop failure in 1521, and France was engaged in disastrous wars.

It is strange, perhaps, that Gil Vicente should have developed out of this sad situation a farcical poem, light and witty. Yet even in the midst of national plight and mourning for royalty, no doubt a lighter moment was at times indicated. The Court may have assembled from time to time, even in its period of mourning, for literary entertainment (*Dom Duardos,* it is to be recalled, may have been read to the Court audience in that year when no dramas were being played). *Maria Parda's Lament,* which is indeed a work of art, may have cheered some otherwise dull hour in the palace, or in a public square.

The literary merit of this "complaint" by Gil Vicente lies principally in the characterization, or caricature, of the protagonist. She is a person, or one of many, whom Gil Vicente may have seen in the Lisbon of his epoch, in the very streets or sections of the city which Maria mentions in her *Lament.* "Besides the life at Court, Gil Vicente seems not to have observed anything more in Lisbon or in the other cities through which he passed," declared António José Saraiva;[7] but this observation of and presentation of a character from lower Lisbon society is one exception at least to Saraiva's general statement. Maria Parda, from among the people, takes her place among the very living creations in Vicente's gallery of portraits. In her overwhelming passion for wine, she sold the last possible of her expendable garments—for example, a mantilla which had cost her two *cruzados*—and having reached the end of all possibilities, came to the last formality in life: her will. In spite of the grotesqueness and the absurd comic nature of her "viciousness," she is a sympathetic person and a very human one.

The text of the dramatic poem appeared in both the 1562 and 1586 editions of the *Copilação*. As proof of a good deal of interest in it, several copies exist, dating from the sixteenth and seventeenth centuries. The oldest copy, in any form, seems to be that owned by the Harvard University Library, a copy which was dated by Braamcamp Freire (*Vida e obras*, p. 382) as belonging to the year of composition, 1522. Luciana Stegagno Picchio used that copy for her critical edition of 1963, but, as she remarks, this dating is not without question. Oscar de Pratt thought highly enough of the *Pranto de Maria Parda* to devote a chapter to it in his previously-mentioned *Gil Vicente: Notas e comentários*. Pratt's feeling is that the poem is close to the *cancioneiro* type of composition at which Anrique da Mota was so skillful, and in which there is a good deal of movement and theater in embryo. (In fact, *Maria Parda* was later carried to the stage in the Teatro Dona Maria in Lisbon, on the occasion of Gil Vicente's fourth centenary, and in it the actress Adelina Ruas gave a superior interpretation.) Indeed, it is to be recalled that Mota's dramatic poems of the decade 1496–1506 had a considerable effect and influence upon the budding Gil Vicente, and this influence may well have been continuing into the time of the *Pranto de Maria Parda*. And if it is an influence to be admitted and recognized, it was not one which was amiss, for the dishevelled and ragged Maria Parda came to be, in the minds of the persons who read of her, the personification of the intoxicated woman, just as Pedreanes (of *The Priest of Beira*) became the symbol of sooth-saying, and Mofina Mendes that of cheerfulness amid misfortune. It was the broad humor of the portrayal, in spite of its tragic undertones, which caught the fancy of the reader, and it made a lasting impression.

These Miscellaneous Works, as has been seen, are extremely varied. It is possible that others which would have added to the variety have been lost. They at least show, from those preserved and printed, that Gil Vicente was a man of great versatility.

CHAPTER 8

Gil Vicente's Songs

A S is evident from the plays presented in the previous chapters, Gil Vicente's theater is a very lyric one indeed. Scattered throughout his dramas are fragments of popular songs, and also about fifty complete songs, in Portuguese, in Spanish, and in a mixture of the two languages. Religious songs,—the paraphrases of psalms, for example—at times include phrases from a Latin original.

Many of the songs in Gil Vicente's plays have been called "traditional," in that some familiar theme has been picked up by the dramatist, and developed by him for his purpose. That purpose is usually to employ the lyrics as part of the dramatic action, but once in a while, as an interruption, for variety's sake, one finds a kind of sung interlude. The characters of the play, it is to be noted, are the persons, in all of the plays, who sing the songs, and the songs are often accompanied by a musical background and the use of a dance. These last attributes—music and dancing—as well as the songs, have caught the attention of several critics; and it is of significance that Braamcamp Freire devoted a chapter to the subject in his often-mentioned definitive monograph on the dramatist.[1] The dances are often named (but at best only slightly described by Gil Vicente), and it has been only possible to "discover the musical versions and the composers of some of those Castilian and Portuguese popular dances and songs which the very rich Peninsular folkloric treasure offered to the Poet, who did not delay in making use of it" (Beau, p. 221).

A very few of the songs in the plays seem to have been composed by Gil Vicente himself. For example, it is stated in the *Copilação* that he purposely composed, for *The Play of the Sibyl Cassandra*, "How comely the maiden, / How lovely and fair!" ("Muy graciosa es la doncella")—Bell, No. 34, pp. 70–71, "feita e

ensoada pelo autor"; for *The Forge of Love,* "Let him come without a fear / Who would his soul's temper prove" ("El que quisiese
apurarse")—Bell, No. 44, pp. 94–95, "cantiga feita pelo autor ao
propósito"; for *The Farce of the Doctors,* "It was in the month of
May . . ." ("En el mes era de maio"), "una ensalada por Gil Vicente guisada"; and for *The History of God,* "Wearily with tears
of anguish, / Prisoners aloud were crying" ("Voces daban prisioneros, / Luengo tiempo están llorando")—Bell, No. 42, pp. 90–91,
"[cantiga] que fez o mesmo autor ao mesmo proposito." But in
every case, whether the songs were original with him or not (and
mostly they were not), "his skill," as Bowra states, "lies in making
these themes his own and working the completed poems into his
plays by many happy and appropriate touches." This inclusion of
lyrics in theater is not a new thing with Gil Vicente, of course; it
had been found, for example, in Juan del Encina and in earlier
French dramatists, as Pierre Le Gentil has pointed out in his very
significant study.

Aubrey F. G. Bell, as has been noted before, gathered together
fifty-one of Gil Vicente's best lyrics, providing the original text on
one page and a fine English translation on the other. In Coimbra,
a few years previously, as noted too, Joaquim Mendes dos Remédios had compiled a collection of "lyric verses or fragments of
songs scattered through Gil Vicente's works." In the mid-thirties,
Dámaso Alonso brought together his "complete edition of the
Castilian lyrics." And very recently indeed, Thomas R. Hart has
published his little volume which includes some of the best of
Vicente's lyrics from the plays, in both Portuguese and Spanish,
and also the verse-sermon of 1506.

All of the critics, dealing with the subject, speak highly of Gil
Vicente as a lyricist: "Gil Vicente was the greatest dramatist of his
country and his time," wrote Bell (*Lyrics*), "but he was, above all,
a great lyric poet. His lyricism, indeed, at its best, and based on
genuine popular poetry, has rarely been surpassed." "One of the
greatest and richest lyric poets of the Castilian language," declared Dámaso Alonso. "His wide understanding of human character and his ready delight in many of its aspects," said Bowra,
"enabled him not only to be a dramatist, but to pass beyond mere
drama to the universal states of mind which lie behind its assump-
tions and conventions. The abundant life which he saw and en-

joyed around him inspired him to ecstatic joy which found its expression in the soaring sweep of irresistible song."

This "irresistible song" was derived from many rich sources of inspiration, and it is Bowra who has classified, in a skilful way, many models from both Portugal and Spain, which Gil Vicente had at his disposal.

I *The* Cossante

One is the Portuguese *cossante*, with examples surviving from as far back as the thirteenth century, which has as the most notable characteristic a refrain. Simple and monotonous, these strictly indigenous little poems have a tone of wistful sadness. Their fresh charm, "which went straight from the field and hill into palace and song-book," as Bell puts it, has been caught by Gil Vicente to a remarkable degree. "White Thou art, white as a lily,/ Virgin most Holy. / In Bethlehem, Our Lady's Bower, / From the Rose was born a Flower, / Virgin most Holy" ("Blanca estais colorada, / Virgem sagrada. / Em Belem, villa do amor / Da rosa nasceu a flor: / Virgem sagrada") are the first two stanzas (which show the repetition) of a beautiful *cossante* sung by the market girls in two alternating choirs at the end of *The Fair* (the English as given is by George Young;[2] see also Bell, No. 2, pp. 4–5). This poem of most graceful mastery is skilful in its use of refrain, and its alternating assonance produces "a slow, unwinding movement suited to the regular movement" of the dance which accompanied the song, as the actors and actresses left the stage in the dénouement of the play.

Another *cossante* (see Bell, No. 16, pp. 32–33), from *The Pastoral Tragicomedy of the Estrêla Mountain Range*, "stands out," says Bell, "like the bough of gold from the surrounding foliage": "A friend of mine, a friend of old, / Sends unto me apples of gold. / So fair is love" ("Um amigo que eu havia / Mançanas d'ouro m'envia, / Garrido amor! / Um amigo que eu amava, / Mançanas d'ouro me manda, / Garrido amor!"). Or, from *The Triumph of Winter*, "a perfect specimen of the *cossante*" (Bell, No. 23, pp. 48–49): "Mother, from where the roses blow, / Red roses blow, come I" ("Del rosal vengo, mi madre, / Vengo del rosale"). All of these, naturally, are more significant when read in their entirety.

The Spanish *villancico,* in which the theme is briefly stated, and then developed in longer stanzas with a repeated refrain, was frequently used by Gil Vicente. A good example is "The falcon that dares / With heron to fight / Has danger in sight" ("Halcón que se atreve / Con garza guerrera / Peligros espera"), from *The Play of Rubena* (Bell, No. 49, pp. 104–105; Alonso, No. 12, p. 33). This song, sung by the needlewomen of Crete, is of a kind which is "a distant but recognizable descendant of the Moorish zéjel," treated with judgment and care, and exploited "with tact and grace" (Bowra).

Another song, classified by the critics simply as a "refrain-song," is a type from early times. Examples go back as far as Aristophanes, and Shakespeare used them in *As You Like It* and in *A Midsummer Night's Dream.* A very fine and representative *refrain* in Gil Vicente is a May-song in *The Play of Lusitania,* where May, the messenger of the Sun, enters singing: "May is here, now May is here, / May is here and all aflower" ("Este é Maio, o Maio é este, / Este é Maio, e florece"). The concentrated and repetitive phraseology is very evident in the complete song (see Bell, No. 1, pp. 2–3). In the building of these "refrain-songs," Gil Vicente seems to have decided upon a "key-line" (drawn from folk-culture probably) and elaborated upon it. "His expansion of a theme," declares Bowra, "is perfectly related to the tone set at the start, even though he puts it in a new context and gives it a reference for which it was not originally intended." A traditional refrain (or *estribillo,* to use the Spanish technical name) seems to have been the starting point for the song of the three sea-nymphs as they enter in *The Play of the Fairies:* "Which of us most wearièd / Has in this long journey sped? / Which of us most wearièd?" ("Qual de nós vem mais cansada / Nesta cansada jornada? / Qual de nós vem mais cansada?"). (For the complete song, to be enjoyed in its full form, see Bell, No. 7, pp. 14–15.)

II *The* Serranilha

The *serranilha* (mountain girl song), found in delightful examples in Gil Vicente's plays, is a lyric of long tradition; existing, for example, in Spain's medieval *Book of Good Love* (*Libro de buen amor*), by the Archpriest of Hita, and in the works of the fifteenth-century Marqués de Santillana. In this conventional and rather artificial poem, the singer meets a beautiful shepherdess in the mountains. He pays her compliments and presses his suit, but she usually rejects his advances and sends him away. One of the best and most popular *serranilhas* in Gil Vicente's works is Pero Vaz's song in *The Farce of the Carriers,* where, as Young puts it, the man from the country relates an amorous adventure "in snatches, interrupted by adjurations to his mules and conversations with other carriers and passers-by": "Cold was the mountain pass, snowy and high, / When I saw a sweet mountainy maiden come by. . . . / I saw a sweet mountainy maiden come by, / And went up to her to speak gallantry. . . . / Mistress, quoth I, wouldst have company, pray? / Master, quoth she, pray pass on your way" ("A serra é alta, fria e nevosa, / Vi venir serrana gentil, graciosa. . . . / Vi venir serrana, gentil, graciosa. / Cheguei-me per'ella, com grã cortesia. . . . / Disse-lhe, senhora, quereis companhia? / Disse-me, escudeiro, segui vossa via").

Eminent Portuguese critics have commented on this delightful poem on many occasions (the English translation above is from Young's *Anthology,* p. 59). A similarity has been pointed out to Guido Cavalcanti's *pastorella,* "E domandai se avesse compagnia / Ed ella mi rispose dolcemente / Che sola sola per lo bosco gia." Bowra contrasts the Vicentine *serranilha* with those of the two famous Spanish poets noted above (the Archpriest of Hita and the Marqués de Santillana) and finds that Gil Vicente's work is superior to those preceding him: "If the first of these displays a pungent, realistic satire and the second a masculine confidence and gaiety, Vicente aims only at poetry. He has reduced his song to the absolute minimum and put into it nothing that is not essential. . . . The first couplet gives the setting, the second the opening move in the knight's progress, the third his stylish gallantry, the fourth his rebuff. All of course lead up to the delightful, humorous, unexpected end and create the atmosphere for it. This is as far from the uncertain touch of popular song as we could wish, and yet it is perfectly fresh and natural."

In *The Triumph of Winter,* the shepherd Juan Guijarro sings and dances to a *serranilha,* in which the dark mountain girl wants the man to stay and keep her company, for she is all alone; and at the end of *The Judge of Beira,* the actors sing a "prelude" to a

mountain-girl song, which promises adventure to come. Delightful compositions all of them.

III   *The Ballad*

The *ballad,* in whatever country it flourishes, has always been a
very popular form of poetry, and the presence of several ballads
on the lips of various characters in Gil Vicente's plays demon-
strated Portugal's continuing interest in the *genre.* We remember
that the chivalrous play, *Dom Duardos,* ended in a beautiful *romance:* "It was in the month of April, / One day from the month
of May. . . ." *The Play of Lusitania* contains a moving lament, in
ballad form, where the Jewish tailor and his son sing, as they sew,
the misfortunes of old Valencia of the time of the eleventh-
century Cid Campeador: "Oh, Valença, woe Valença! / Thou
shalt burn with fire anon, / For thou wast a Moorish city / Ere
by Christians thou wert won" ("Ai Valença, guai Valença, / De
fogo sejas queimada, / Primeiro foste de moiros / Que de christi-
anos tomada"). In this ballad (the English version given here is
by Young, p. 11; Bell has a different rendering, No. 20, pp.
40–41), a Moor is berating the Mediterranean city for having
been a turncoat, from the Mohammedan to the Christian side, in
the Peninsula's long medieval War of Reconquest (711–1492).

The departure of young Princess Beatriz (almost 17) for Italy,
in August, 1521, to marry the Duke of Savoy, was the occasion, as
is well known, for a palace celebration in which Gil Vicente presented his *Courts of Jupiter.* This play includes a contemporary
ballad, pertinent to the situation, which both Bell (No. 39, pp.
80–81) and Alonso (No. 20, p. 45) have chosen for their collec-
tions: "Young and fair was the Infanta, / And her name was Bea-
trice, / Grand-daughter of King Ferdinand, / The best of all Kings
of Castille, / Daughter of King Manuel / And Doña Maria the
Queen" ("Niña era la infanta, / Doña Beatriz se dezía, / Nieta
del buen Rey Hernando, / El mejor Rey de Castilla, / Hija del
Rey don Manuel / Y Reyna doña María"). This ballad was sung
in chorus by the signs and planets in the play, and it must have
deeply moved the Court as their beloved Princess, of tender years,
was on the point of departure for distant parts.

Past and present glories of Portugal caught the fancy of Gil

Vicente in another ballad, sung by the sirens in *The Triumph of Winter:* "God of Heaven, King of Earth, / Thou for ever praisèd be, / Since Thy great might Thou hast shown / In all things that were made by Thee" ("Dios del cielo, Rey del mundo, / Por siempre seas loado, / Que mostraste tus grandezas / En todo quanto has criado")—the texts are in Bell, No. 40, pp. 82–83 and Alonso, No. 24, p. 51. This patriotic synthesis of the history of Portugal in the form of an old ballad goes on to praise the first king of Portugal, Afonso Henriques, the later Portuguese achievements in the East, and finally the contemporary king, João III. Once more Gil Vicente was revealing himself to be truly the poet laureate of his nation.

IV *Gil Vicente's Variety in Song*

Variety is the keynote in these songs of Gil Vicente. From an awe-inspiring psalm such as "Praise the Lord on high, / Spirits of the Blest" ("O devotas almas felis, / Per sempre sem cessar / *Laudate Dominum de coelis*")—Bell, No. 9, pp. 18–19, sung by the Virgin, Prudence, and Humility in *The Play of Mofina Mendes*); or a *Te Deum,* "Worthy of adoration, Thee, / O Lord, our God, we praise" ("A ti, dino de adorar, / A ti, nuestro Dios, loamos")— Bell, No. 25, pp. 52–53, sung by the angels at the birth of Jesus in *The Play of the Four Seasons;* to moving love songs such as "From my Love they me would part, / From my Love so fair" ("Apartarme-ão de vós, / Garrido Amor!")—Bell, No. 13, pp. 26–27, sung by the poverty-stricken squire Aires Rosado in *Who Has Bran?; from* stately verses in praise of a new-born prince such as "Twas in May, the month of May, / Eight days ere it ended be, / When the Infante Don Felipe / Was born in Evora city. / Hurrah! Hurrah!" ("Por Maio era por Maio, / Ocho días por andar, / El Iffante Don Felipe / Nació en Evora ciudad. / Huha! Huha!)—Bell, No. 22, pp. 44–45, Alonso, No. 26, p. 56, from *The Pilgrimage of the Aggrieved,* performed in Evora, in 1533, to celebrate this event, or in celebration of a royal marriage, such as "Now'll Castille exult in glee, / For a queen so fair to see" ("Pardeos, bem andou Castella, / Pois tem Rainha tão bella!")—Bell, No. 21, pp. 42–43, from *The Temple of Apollo,* sung by the dancing pilgrims to celebrate the marriage of Princess Isabel to the Emperor Charles V in 1526; from a simple *vilancete* such as "Though life be full of sorrow, /

Yet never hope be lost" ("Por mais que la vida pene, / No se pierde el esperanza")—Bell, No. 36, pp. 74–75, sung by the three sirens as they come on stage in *The Triumph of Winter*, to a more artificial courtly lyric such as "Now no more my Lady wills / That I speak with her alone" ("Já não quer minha Senhora / Que lhe falle em apartado")—Bell, No. 12, pp. 24–25, sung by Lopo, as he dances, in *The Pastoral Tragicomedy of the Estrêla Mountain Range*, or "Consolation, get thee gone, / Since my torture thou mayst see" ("Consuelo, vete con Dios; / Pues ves la vida que sigo")—Bell, No. 24, pp. 50–51, Alonso, No. 13, p. 34, sung by the courtier, Dario, to the accompaniment of his viola in *The Play of Rubena*—all of these Gil Vicente handled with skill and originality, in a manner befitting a great lyricist. And to prove that he wrote songs in a manner befitting a great dramatist, it is sufficient to include a couple of examples sung to the accompaniment of dramatic action, such as, "Very tranquil lies the sea, / Rowers, to your places move!" ("Mui serena está la mar, / A los remos, remadores!")—Bell, No. 32, pp. 66–67, Alonso, No. 17, p. 40, where in *The Ship of Love*, the "fidalgos" are busily caulking a miniature ship on stage as they sing; and the previously mentioned refrain-song, "Let him come without fear / Who would his soul's temper prove / To this forge, the forge of Love" ("El que quisiere apurarse, / Véngase muy sin temor / A la fragoa del Amor")— Bell, No. 44, pp. 94–95, Alonso, No. 18, p. 42, which is a real anvil chorus, in *The Forge of Love*.

Harvey L. Johnson, in his article on "Longfellow and Portuguese Language and Literature," [3] has pointed out that the American poet and professor of modern languages at Harvard College revealed in his translations and literary studies "his perception of the beauties of Portuguese poetry." In *The Poets and Poetry of Europe*, Longfellow included his own translation of a song by Gil Vicente:

> If thou art sleeping, maiden,
>   Awake and open thy door:
> 'T is the break of day, and we must away,
>   O'er meadow, and mount, and moor.
>
> Wait not to find thy slippers,
>   But come with thy naked feet:

We shall have to pass through the dewy grass,
And waters wide and fleet.

("Si dormís, doncella,
  Despertad y abrid.
  Que venida es la hora
  Si queréis partir.
  Si estáis descalza,
  Não curéis de vos calzar,
  Que muchas aguas
  Tenéis de pasar.")

This song, which is sung by Aires Rosado in *Who Has Bran?* to his lady, Isabel, amid the barking of neighborhood dogs, appears in Alonso, No. 27, p. 59, and in a different English version in Bell, No. 38, pp. 78–79.

Back in 1835, Longfellow had translated the very lyrical "Muy graciosa es la doncella," from *The Play of the Sibyl Cassandra,* and had called the song "a little ditty . . . as delicate as a dewdrop." In his *Poets and Poetry of Europe,* he had used, however, a translation by John Bowring, but later returned to his own superior rendering, which is worth reproducing:

She is a maid of artless grace,
Gentle in form, and fair of face.

Tell me, thou ancient mariner,
    That sailest on the sea,
If ship, or sail, or evening star
    Be half as fair as she!

Tell me, thou gallant cavalier,
    Whose shining arms I see,
If steed, or sword, or battlefield
    Be half so fair as she!

Tell me, thou swain, that guard'st thy flock
    Beneath the shadowy tree,
If flock, or vale, or mountain-ridge
    Be half so fair as she!

("Muy graciosa es la doncella:
Como es bella y hermosa!

Digas tú, el marinero,
Que en las naves vivías,
Si la nave o la vela o la estrella
Es tan bella.

Digas tú, el caballero,
Que las armas vestías,
Si el caballo o las armas o la guerra
Es tan bella.

Digas tú, el pastorcico,
Que el ganadico guardas,
Si el ganado o los valles o la sierra
Es tan bella.")

"Longfellow," wrote Harvey Johnson, "translated both of Gil Vicente's little compositions with accuracy, adhering to their original form and sense and preserving their simplicity and charm. The two renditions are extremely successful in catching the essence of what the Portuguese poet wrote and there is little, if any, loss in melody or evocative power." To Longfellow, to Young, and to Bell, especially, go gratitude for making a considerable number of these fine Vicentine poems available to the English-reading public.

These songs in Gil Vicente's plays, let it be repeated, are closely connected with the dramatic action. Rarely indeed, if ever, is a lyric entirely disconnected. Very often the songs are accompanied by dancing, and usually one or more musical instruments are being played. Sometimes one singer is involved, but frequently several or a chorus carry the melody. Simplicity is a constant attribute, as Gil Vicente skilfully handles these traditional popular meters on the eve of a period of elaboration. By the mid-twenties, we recall, the poet Sá de Miranda had returned from Italy with the hendecasyllabic line, with its various strophes such as sonnets, octaves, tercets, etc., but Gil Vicente stood firm in his unsophisticated, medieval position to combat the growing literary artificialities at Court. The Italian meters would win out in due time, but the rustic native lines, looked upon with contempt by the innovators, held fast their position as long as Gil Vicente's authoritative practice continued. But after him, as far as lyrics were concerned, he could have said, in a different sense, with a later French king: "Après moi, le déluge."

CHAPTER 9

Gil Vicente the Impresario

I N *A Play by Gil Vicente* (*Um Auto de Gil Vicente*), of the year 1838, by the nineteenth-century romantic dramatist, Almeida Garrett, Gil Vicente is presented to the public as the actor-director of a theatrical company at the Court of King Manuel. In this play he is busy preparing for and putting on the performance of *The Courts of Jupiter* to celebrate (as has been noted on several occasions before) the departure of Princess Beatriz for Savoy in 1521. In the hands of the romantic writer, some three hundred years after the event, facts are distorted (for example, the supposed love of the poet Bernardim Ribeiro for the departing Princess becomes the main point of the drama); but nevertheless Gil Vicente, the Court impresario, is no doubt correctly portrayed in his functions as they were in reality in the years 1502–1536.

Almeida Garrett gives at some length the preparations for the palace evening party (*serão*) held immediately before the royal group embarked at Lisbon on the 1000-ton *Sancta Catherina de Monte Sinai*. In this nineteenth-century *auto*, Gil Vicente is calling together his actors and actresses for a rehearsal (his own daughter Paula is playing the part of Providence; Gil Vicente himself is Jupiter). Later, we see the Court assembled for the performance itself. The portion of *The Courts of Jupiter* which Almeida Garrett's audience witnesses is the final scene where a Moorish girl presents Princess Beatriz with gifts. In the Almeida Garrett romantic version, the enamored Bernardim stealthily assumes this rôle and, instead of saying the words as prepared by Gil Vicente, pours out to the Princess his love and his despair at her leaving him. At this, Beatriz faints, and the Vicentine play, in a romanticized version, ends in a certain confusion. Then King Manuel, trying to cover up a suspicious, involved situation, declares: "Our Gil Vicente was not happy this time in the dénouement of his play. He usually ends on a happier note. Let us go to the next chamber, and be cheered up with dancing, for the play has left us somewhat sad." [1]

There is nothing of this "romantic" implication in the Vicentine *Courts of Jupiter,* of course. The play does end with the usual singing and dancing, but there is no indication as to who played what parts; nor is there any reference whatsoever to the legendary love affair between the poet Bernardim Ribeiro and King Manuel's youthful daughter. Bernardim Ribeiro (1482–1552) went on to become secretary to King João III in 1524; but a hopeless passion for an unidentified lady did drive him from the Court, and finally to an insane asylum. However, as Aubrey F. G. Bell tells us,[2] any reference to Princess Beatriz "is now definitely discarded." Princess Beatriz sailed, without any mishap, to Savoy, married the Duke, and while she died at the age of 34 (1504–1538), she was the ancestor of many members of the Italian royal family.

Interestingly enough, there is one contemporary account of that evening in the Royal Palace in Lisbon, in August, 1521, before Beatriz embarked on her voyage by sea. For Gil Vicente, this seems to be the only description of its kind extant, and we owe it to the poet-historian Garcia de Resende (c. 1470–1536), the compiler of the *Cancioneiro Geral* (or *Cancioneiro de Resende*), of 1516, and secretary to João II and to King Manuel. His words run as follows: "In a very large drawing room, richly adorned with tapestries of gold, well carpeted, and with canopy, chairs, and cushions of rich brocade, there began a great ball in which the King our Lord danced with the Lady Infanta Duchess his daughter. . . . And when the dances were over, there began a very good and well devised play with many well adorned and very natural figures, a performance very well arranged and à propos; and when the play was over, the evening party came to an end." [3]

Laurence Keates (p. 96) points out the Resende's brief and cryptic description "tells us three very important things about the production as such. It was a *cousa muito bem ordenada,* which is tantamount to saying that the production was very competent. The characters were costumed with care, and were also *mui naturaes.* . . . From [the last phrase], we conclude that Vicente's actors were presenting the work in a polished and convincing

manner. They had been well rehearsed." Nevertheless, in spite of
the excellence usually achieved, Braamcamp Freire reminds us
(*Vida e obras,* p. 41) that Gil Vicente's dramatic productions did
not require a long time in preparation. "He conceived them either
through his own initiative or through someone else's suggestion,
and put them on." Proof of this short period spent in preparation
exists in the case of *The Pastoral Tragicomedy of the Estrêla
Mountain Range,* which was put on to celebrate the birth of Princess Maria in Coimbra, on October 15, 1527. There are lines composed between the hour of the Queen's delivery and the almost-
immediately following Court performance. The Mountain Range
(Serra da Estrêla) declares that she is overjoyed at the birth of the
Princess and mentions that the new-born baby was born on a
Tuesday. "Indeed," says Braamcamp Freire "the Princess' birthday was on that day of the week." It is conceivable, of course, that
Gil Vicente, well aware of the impending birth in the royal household, may have had a play pretty well ready, and touched it up in
several places to make it completely fit the event.

In the physical presentation of these plays, Gil Vicente was
working under very rudimentary and primitive conditions. There
was not any regularly constituted or developed stage as we know
it. Gil Vicente was usually putting on his pieces, at the king's command, in a hall or in the chapel of a royal palace. And it was
simply that, and no more. The actors were not performing on a
raised platform, but on the floor of the room, the "stage" being on
the same plane as the spectators. The audience was seated around
the place of action, with the king and queen, and other privileged
members of the Court, perhaps, sitting on a dais. "This particular
arrangement," as Laurence Keates says, "would have suited the
proprieties of the *serão* (evening party): the play was an integral
part of the evening's entertainment, presided over by the monarch."

The stage directions of the 1562 *Copilação* provide a good
many simple suggestions as to the action on the stage. However,
these written directions must be taken with some caution, since
they may have been added, or added to, at any rate, by the son
Luis as he prepared the volume for the printer. (Carolina Michaëlis de Vasconcelos, however, in her *Notas Vicentinas,* I,
thinks that these indications are worthy of credence, having been

inspired at least by Gil Vicente himself.) There is nothing involved in most cases, and the general simplicity and rudimentary nature of the stage actions must have been the dramatist's procedure, if not his written instruction. A good example of this practical simplicity is to be found in the directions for the presentation of the nativity scene in *The Sibyl Cassandra:* "Curtains are opened, and the *crèche* appears." The play was first presented in a side chapel of the Convent of Enxobregas, Lisbon. Nothing is more natural than to have used the cradle and the attendant figures already set up for the Christmas season. The crib, or manger scenes, so frequently found in Gil Vicente's plays (in *The Castilian Pastoral Play, The Play of the Magi, The Play of the Four Seasons, The Play of Mofina Mendes,* etc., etc.) would have been very easy to arrange.

Ronald B. Williams, as has been noted before, has studied in detail the stage presentation of Vicente's plays. Williams stresses a characteristic already mentioned: utter simplicity, on most occasions; and also the fact that Gil Vicente was very skilful in giving a visual suggestion, or impression, of the setting. In *The Play of Fame,* for example, "the impression of a country scene is created by the mention of geese, meadow, *ribera* (bank), and country house. The house seems to lie on a road along which pass a Frenchman, an Italian and a Castilian who successively pay court to the Glory of Portugal personified in a young girl and are rejected by her." Reference to flocks in *The Pastoral Tragicomedy of the Estrêla Mountain Range* implies an outdoor place; and outdoor places in the hills are at least implied in other plays such as *The Play on the Coat of Arms of the City of Coimbra* and *The Play of the Canaanite Woman.* In *The Forest of Deceits,* it is interesting to note that "a single, simple scene represents a succession of places [shop, palace, countryside, a house, a mountain]. Transition [from one place to another] is indicated by means of an empty stage, and by statements of characters relative to place." That "the scenery must have been largely conjured up in the dialogue" can be taken as a very general and usual occurrence. And it is worth stressing, when thinking of possible influences of Gil Vicente upon later Peninsular drama, that this conjuring up of place, through the words of the actors and actresses, was a strong point in the *comedia* of the seventeenth-century Spaniard, Lope de Vega.

Sometimes, however, there was a certain elaborateness attempted in the stage setting. The *Barcas* trilogy is a good example of this. *The Ship of Hell* makes use of two boats, which must have appeared realistically on the stage. The orders which are given by the Devil of the boat destined for Hell point to a fully-equipped sailing vessel: "He orders the tightening and loosening of halyards, the fixing of a clew, the lowering of the breech, the raising of the yard, and the preparation of anchor, flags, rower's bench, and stern deck" (Williams), with numerous references to the gangplank. No doubt the other *Ships* too used boats on the stage, and stage properties of all of them are numerous, but of easy provenance: the usurer's large purse, the shoemaker's last, the friar's sword and shield, the procuress' bag of cosmetics, the Jew's goat and coins, the magistrate's documents, the peasant's plow, the angels' sail bearing the device of a crucifix, the oars of Christ, etc., etc.

Play after play makes use of simple props which, in his rôle as actor-manager, must have been easily available to Gil Vicente. A shepherdess of *The Portuguese Pastoral Play*, for example, is carrying a bundle of firewood; in *The Priest of Beira*, the peasant boy is carrying a basket of provisions; in *The Fair*, a stand or display counter is used, as the title implies; in *The Soul's Journey*, it is a table, with four dishes containing the food of the Passion; in *The Forest of Deceits*, it is a store equipped with chairs and display windows. As for musical instruments, for example in *The Courts of Jupiter* trumpets are blown by the four Winds, and in *The Play of the Doctors*, a guitar is played. In *Amadis de Gaula* and in *The Play of the Doctors*, letters are handed around; in *The Play of the Fairies*, slips of paper bearing fortunes are drawn by the King's guests. The religious plays, in addition to portraying the common nativity scene, mentioned previously, or having other common pious stage properties, may have, for example, a bier bearing the image of the dead Christ, as in *The History of God*. For *The Judge of Beira*, it would not have been difficult to find the necessary seat with back rest and a bench; for *Amadis de Gaula*, it may have been more difficult to simulate an orchard and a pond, unless, as may have been true for *Dom Duardos,* a palace garden may have been the actual place of performance.

Flowers are a common prop: in *Dom Duardos,* Camilote places a wreath of roses on Maimonda's head; in *The Old Man of the Orchard,* flowers, and in particular a rose, are needed. In *The Coat of Arms of the City of Coimbra,* a lion and a serpent (part of the coat of arms of the city) appear in some form or other. There is no indication as to how these animals were represented, and one might ask whether the above-mentioned goat led by the Jew in *The Ship of Hell* was really a live one. The realistic animal effects, in a night scene in *Who Has Bran?*—the barking of a dog, the meowing of a cat, the crowing of a rooster—all occur off-stage. The realism of boats has already been mentioned: in *The Ship of Hell* "so represented that passengers may embark and still be visible to the audience" (Williams). The vessel of *The Ship of Love* is only a miniature one, but one which is realistically fitted out. In *The Forge of Love,* the castle seems to be small in scale, but the forge was no doubt full-fledged. Real foliage of bushes and trees seems to have increased the life-likeness of both *The Portuguese Pastoral Play* and *The Priest of Beira.*

"The position of Gil Vicente at the King's Court enabled him," wrote Williams, "to enrich his scene with large and small devices and properties. He also made generous use of costumes to show the rank or occupation of his characters. Dress appropriate to an allegorical figure, peasant, widower, courtier, pilgrim, gardener, friar, king, magistrate, shepherdess, or queen is usually specified." From the first dramatic presentation, the *Monólogo do Vaqueiro* of 1502, where Gil Vicente was alone on the "stage," dressed as a herdsman, through *The Castilian Pastoral Play, The Play of the Magi,* etc., etc., up to and including the final *Forest of Deceits* of 1536, the shepherd or shepherdess, dressed no doubt in simple but realistic rustic costume, is a frequent and important figure. But there is a host of others, all bearing some distinctive item of their occupation or position in society. The Chief Justice of the last-mentioned play naturally wears the cassock of his office and a magistrate's robe and gloves. In *The Pilgrimage of the Aggrieved,* Frei Paço, holding court, wears the robes of his religious order, with hood, velvet cap, gloves and a golden sword. In *The Play of* the Four Seasons, Summer is appropriately distinguished from the other seasons by the wearing of a straw hat. Other significant touches are frequently found: in *The Triumph of Winter,* for example, the misery of the poverty-stricken shepherd is indicated by having him wear only one shoe; a poor old woman is traveling about with bare feet. The Blessed Virgin, on the other hand, in *The Play of Mofina Mendes,* is dressed as a queen, in a manner befitting the Queen of Heaven.

Characters in disguise have, naturally, to wear a double costume: Prince Rosvel of *The Play of the Widower* is covered with servant's livery before removing it to reveal, at the proper time, his princely garments. Dom Duardos, in his rôle of pretense, appears in gardener's clothes, to later come before us in finery befitting his station in life. In *The Play of the Widower* too, it is clearly indicated that the two daughters go off stage to return dressed in festive costumes for their marriages with the princes.

Allegorical figures, supernatural figures, and historical-legendary figures are very common, as is well known, in the Vicente theater, and no doubt the dramatist clothed those figures in the manner which would make them and their significance immediately clear to the audience. In the plays there is little indication, as far as detail goes, of what that costuming was; but doubtless those witnessing the dramatic piece held a common idea of what an angel, a devil, etc., looked like, and how he should be presented. In *The Play of Faith,* according to the shepherd Benito's words, Faith is dressed, curiously enough, in Moorish style (*a la morisca*). David is dressed in shepherd's costume (*em figura de pastor*) in *The Courts of Jupiter.* Providence is described, in the stage directions in the same play, as "a princess, with a sphere and sceptre in her hand." The four winds appear as trumpeters, but no suggestion is made as to the costuming of the Sun and Moon, who enter dancing to the sound of the trumpets. Portuguese Fame, in *The Play of Fame,* appears in the figure of a peasant girl from the Province of Beira, watching her ducks; but no guidance is given as to the dress of her suitors (the Frenchman, the Italian and the Spaniard). Perhaps their "fractured" language was sufficient to indicate their country of origin, without any particular costuming being necessary. Faith and Fortitude, in the same play, are not described as to dress; but once again it might be said that they were probably clothed in a traditional, medieval way with which the audience was well acquainted.

In *The Forge of Love,* the four Planets are richly adorned mountain girls, whose costumes are covered with stars, according to the 1562 stage directions. Justice is an old hunchbacked woman, blind in one eye, shabbily dressed, and with a broken wand! In *The Temple of Apollo,* World appears as a "pilgrim"; in *The History of God,* World appears dressed as a king. In the indications given in the 1562 edition, Portugal, of *The Play of Lusitania,* wears a hunter's costume; in *The Play of the Canaanite Woman,* the three Laws (of Nature, of Scripture, and of Grace) are represented as shepherdesses. In the final play, *The Forest of Deceits,* Fortune, and several other characters, are "pilgrims."

María Rosa Lida de Malkiel, in her study of the genesis of *The Sibyl Cassandra,* previously mentioned, objects to some modern conclusions drawn about costuming in the stage productions of Gil Vicente's plays. Her examples are naturally from the play which she is studying in detail. To her mind, the conclusion (as presented by some earlier critics and by Hart) that Cassandra and Solomon were dressed as shepherd and shepherdess respectively is erroneous. Hart and some others before him believed that "their real identity was made clear through allegorical allusions," but María Rosa states that "The probable thing is that each character was wearing the conventional costume [of a sibyl and of a prince] which had been fixed centuries before, and which permitted the immediate recognition of the character." In support of her convincing arguments María Rosa refers back to the monograph by Georgiana Goddard King, who is of her opinion. In fact, Miss King would go so far as to claim that the costuming available might have influenced the play itself: "It is more than probable . . . that the rich and characteristic costumes of the actors, of prophets and sibyls, were the property of the monastery, laid up for use annually among copes and chasubles of many colours and devices; and that the presence of these determined for the ready-witted poet the precise form of his pastoral." The rubric of 1562 does state that the sibyls enter dancing "in the manner of peasant girls," but this means, according to Miss King, "almost certainly that they bear some sign of their rustic occupations, like figures in the Calendars of the *Book of Hours*, basket or hoe or milk-pail; but if they are not recognizable as sibyls by their dress, how is the audience to know them?" In other words, these costumes, "both characteristic and important," came from a long medieval tradition, as is apparent from documents and illustrations of the Middle Ages, and it is very likely indeed, as Georgiana Goddard King and María Rosa Lida de Malkiel believe, that Gil Vicente was not breaking the tradition.

It is worth while noticing in these general considerations of stage-craft in the Vicentine plays, that Gil Vicente may have attempted the use of a "double" stage, or a "divided" stage, in a few cases. *Who Has Bran?* portrays the servants *outside* and Ayres Rosado *inside;* both elements being seen simultaneously by the audience. In *The Play of India,* the stage seems to show a bedroom with a bed, and at the same time the exterior of the house with a doorway. Likewise, in *The Farce of Inês Pereira,* there is an inside room and, at the same time, the exterior of the house with a doorway or doorways. The same seems to hold true for *The Play of Rubena, Dom Duardos,* and *Amadis de Gaula.* But as has been previously indicated, Gil Vicente usually worked on the principle of movement from one place to another throughout a play, and he usually indicated that change by references in the dialogue. The fact that a fair amount of time might elapse in a play certainly required, at times, a suggested change in scenery. For example, about three years elapse in *The Play of India* (from the time of the husband's departure until his return); and in *The Play of Rubena,* which is the most extreme in the passage of time, five years elapse in scene two, and ten years pass between scenes two and three. It is no wonder then that implied changes in setting, through any device possible at the time, were in order.

It is clear from a survey of Gil Vicente's activities as an impresario that throughout the years 1502 to 1536, "the Court did not have a birthday, a marriage or any other important event to celebrate that it did not ask Gil Vicente for a play" (*Obras completas,* I, xiv). It is only necessary to cast one's mind back over Gil Vicente's life story to realize that Marques Braga's statement is correct. After the successful dramatic monologue of 1502, as is known very well, Vicente prepared for the dowager Queen Leanor's Christmas festivities, *The Castilian Pastoral Play;* for her also, for the Epiphany following, *The Play of the Magi;* and for her too, for Corpus Christi of 1504, *The Play of St. Martin.* To drum up enthusiasm for the departure of the Portuguese fleet against Azamor in 1513, apparently, it was *The Exhortation to War;* to celebrate victories in the Far East in the period around 1515 he prepared *The Play of Fame.* For the consolation of the ailing Queen Maria, he put on, in Portuguese, in 1516, *The Ship of Hell;* to please King Manuel's new Queen Leanor, from Spain, *The Ship of Heaven,* in Spanish, in 1519. For the departure of Princess Beatriz for Savoy, it was the frequently-mentioned *Courts of Jupiter.*

When King João III was betrothed to Princess Catarina, sister of the Emperor Charles V, Gil Vicente presented, as we know, *The Forge of Love* (1524). *Dom Duardos* may have been produced for the betrothal of the Emperor to King João's sister in 1525. *The Ship of Love* welcomed Catarina to Lisbon in 1527, *The Triumph of Winter* celebrated the birth of Princess Isabel in April, 1529, and *The Play of Lusitania* celebrated the birth of an heir to the throne in 1532. *The Pilgrimage of the Aggrieved* welcomed the arrival of the new Prince Felipe in 1533, and the last play too, *The Forest of Deceits,* was a Court production in Evora in 1536.

In addition to these Court or Court-chapel plays, Gil Vicente sometimes, but rarely, was called on to serve others: *The Play of the Canaanite Woman,* it will be recalled, was written at the request of the Abbess of Oudivellas and acted in her convent near Lisbon in 1534. One play, *Love's Jubilee,* which is not extant, was produced in the house of the Portuguese ambassador in Brussels, in 1531. *The Festival Play* seems to have been given in a private house. There were no constituted theaters for the people, and one may very well wonder what dramatic entertainment was theirs. António Ribeiro Chiado's *Play of Natural Invention* (*Auto da Natural Invenção*), of about the year 1550, contains a description which proves that the populace was keen on such performances. "So great is the interest," comments Bell (*Four Plays,* p. xxvii), "that not only is the house crowded (where a play is being given) and its door besieged, but the throng in the street outside is so thick that the players have much difficulty in forcing their way through it." The people must have had some contact with the Vicentine plays, for a note in the *Copilação* of 1562 states that the title *Who Has Bran?* was given to the play *by the people* (*vulgo*). (The Vicentine title may have been *The Poor Squire* or *The Squires,* as Marques Braga suggests.) Similarly, it is thought that Gil Vicente's original name for *The Play of Mofina Mendes* was *The Play of the Mysteries of the Virgin,* and his name for *The Priest of Beira, The Play of Pedreanes.* In all of this, Bell (*Four Plays,* p. xxvii) wisely decides: "Therefore when we come upon a new title of a Vicente play unknown to us, we need not conclude that it is a new play."

Gil Vicente's exact position at Court (aside from the goldsmith problem) has been discussed at great length by the critics. Charles E. Nowell's opinion is that, among his functions, he served as "pageant director" and "master of festivities for the Court." [4] We know that this was very true, for in addition to writing his plays for specific occasions, Vicente was sent, for example, from Evora to Lisbon (November 29, 1520) "to prepare for the entry of the King and Queen into their capital (January, 1521)." This was only one of his many activities which have been revealed in connection with all of his dramatic activity. Gil Vicente enjoyed, as has been apparent, the protection and approval of the reigning monarchs of Portugal, and it is apparent, also, that he had sufficient influence to be rather outspoken in his criticism of the political, social and religious conditions of the day. This criticism was received, it seems, in good grace, and Gil Vicente stayed in Court favor until the end of his career.

Author, director, and stage manager, Gil Vicente was also at times an actor. For example, we remember that he was active in the plays of the Spanish *début,* and it has been suggested that from time to time during his career he took other parts; for example, the rôle of Amadis in *Amadis de Gaula.* He was a musician, and the selector of music too, of no mean ability, as Albin Eduard Beau has shown. Above all, let us say that he was a very practical man of the theater, in every possible way. He thrived on the intimate contact with the players of his company and with the audience of the Royal Court. Indeed the intimate relationship between the author-director-actor and his audience was the mainspring of his activity, and it was that coupled with his innate dramatic genius which produced for him such enduring success during his whole literary life.

CHAPTER 10

Limitations and Achievements

I Gil Vicente, the Medievalist

GIL VICENTE was thoroughly medieval in outlook. Untouched by the rebirth of knowledge and the introduction of foreign cultural "progress" which was reaching his native land, he stood aloof from the Renaissance in his "good old ways" to continue medievalism, in its best sense, in all of his activities. As far as theater was concerned, it is Gino Saviotti's considered opinion that "Gil Vicente was not ignorant of this [new theatrical current of the Renaissance] even before Sá de Miranda's return to Portugal in 1526." "We have," concludes Saviotti, "quite a few indications to think that Gil Vicente purposely rejected [the new current]." [1]

As José António Saraiva noted rightly in his study of the dramatist and the Middle Ages, [2] the dramatist was intimately linked with what had preceded him, and not with what was to come after (his influence was, however, considerable on the later Spanish theater and on the later poetry of a popular nature in the Peninsula). Although Saraiva modified his unilateral theory to some extent in later years, [3] seeing Gil Vicente as rather "a reflection of the crisis" between the end of the Middle Ages and the beginning of the Renaissance; and although a case has been made, unsuccessfully, for this same theory by other critics such as Albin Eduard Beau, [4] Gil Vicente remains medieval to the core, and as such he must be judged. It is true that he has been called a humanist at times, but he is that only in the sense that he was deeply interested in humanity and sympathetic toward his fellow beings, as can be seen in his defense of the "New Christians" at the time of the Santarém earthquake of 1531, and in his constant understanding treatment of the characters in his plays. [5]

It is no wonder that Gil Vicente was very medieval indeed. In those last years of the fifteenth century when his philosophy of life and his conception of theater were being formed, and, in the early years of the sixteenth century when his dramatic pieces were being written and performed, his nation had not yet shaken off her ties with the past. The tide was turning and the tone of life was about to be altered (to paraphrase Huizinga's references to France and the Netherlands for the fifteenth century), "but the diapason of life had not yet changed. Scholastic thought, with symbolism, and strong formalism, the thoroughly dualistic conception of life and the world still dominated. . . ." While most of the rest of Europe was turning wholeheartedly to classical forms and concepts of art, Portugal was still in full enjoyment of her medieval tradition. Drama in Portugal was not standing on its own feet with a truly literary purpose, but was still only a part of an evening's (or a day's) entertainment. The end was simply to amuse, to satirize the customs of the people and the failings of the backsliding servants of the Church, or to present religious beliefs or dogmas—all in a very primitive, rudimentary way. The Duke and Duchess of Alba, in Spain, had kept Juan del Encina (and later Lucas Fernández) very busy in providing plays for palace festivities, and the sovereigns of Portugal likewise kept their Court impresario quite occupied in preparing the dramatic performances which whiled away many an hour.

The lack of a unity of action has been a usual and justified criticism directed against the Vicentine theater, and while there may be a deeper unity present at times, still the plays are generally episodic, anecdotal, and novelistic, with insufficient motivation to explain the next event, and without sufficient enchainment to bind events together properly. Indeed one sometimes feels that two almost disconnected plays are being put on under one title, but it is to be remembered that, as Charlotte Stern has pointed out,[6] the majority of Juan del Encina's plays were performed in pairs, and this "pairing" may have influenced Gil Vicente to a great extent as he followed his Salamancan master. Also, variety was no doubt the most sought-after virtue in Court entertainment, and a bipartite play certainly provides that variety.

Holger Sten, referring to Beau's article on the medieval-Renaissance aspects, points out that Gil Vicente lacks other attributes considered desirable in drama in modern times.[7] For example, there is a great deal of variety of movement, but no real dramatic action; the interrelationships of persons are varied and multifold, but there are no real conflicts; there is plenty of surprise, for the unexpected does occur with frequency, but there is little dramatic tension; in short, the plays are structurally "undramatic," containing, however, many small scenes in themselves perfect.[8]

II *Theater as Entertainment*

On the positive side, Gil Vicente possessed, in his primitive and rudimentary way, a keen sense of theater as entertainment. He was "the greatest comic poet which the World has seen in the long period of 1800 years, from Plautus to Molière," claims J. A. Pires de Lima.[9] And he was, in spite of his many shortcomings, when his plays are criticized through twentieth-century eyes, a very successful dramatist writing for a living stage before an alert, but perhaps uncritical, audience. A feature with him was audience participation, in an undeveloped theatrical setting which provided the greatest proximity between the players and the audience. In Vicente's first dramatic effort, it is to be recalled, the King and Queen were silent participants in the action, and in some later plays, members of the audience played rôles even vocally.

Gil Vicente knew other tricks of the trade to make the plays more interesting. Just as the audience's imagination would be drawn upon a century later in the Spanish *comedia* to visualize the setting with a minimum of stage props, so Gil Vicente very frequently evoked vivid visual impressions. We remember, for example that on one occasion, by having the characters mention a meadow, geese, a country house, etc., that effect was brought about. Changes in setting within a play were normally accomplished in the same manner, in the speeches of the characters—a device also constantly employed later in the Spanish theater. A technique, by coincidence extremely modern, occurs in *Who Has Bran?*, when Aires Rosado is serenading his Isabel at her window. The heroine speaks in such a low voice that the audience must guess her words, but guess them it can from the hero's reactions. Twentieth-century plays use this method in "telephone scenes," and it may have been an invention of Gil Vicente's very own.[10]

Gil Vicente was a splendid lyric poet, in a traditional, popular way, as has been seen by frequent reference to this outstanding quality, and by the dedication of a complete chapter to his "songs." It is without any doubt true that, as Bell has told us (*Gil Vicente*, p. 16), Gil Vicente "had a lyrical gift surpassed by very few poets of any age or country." His verse forms in the plays were almost always the old meters drawn from medieval Portugal and Spain, and his songs (within the plays also) were usually adaptations of folkloric elements. He was the first, Eugenio Asensio believes (*Itinerario del entremés*, p. 72, note), to use the ballad meter (the old eight-syllable *versos de romance*) for dialogue (it was thus used in the last scene of *Dom Duardos*). Lope de Vega, the greatest exponent of the *comedia*, made good and frequent use of this meter for this purpose in Spain a century afterwards. Likewise in Spain's seventeenth century, *The Sibyl Cassandra's* compression of history and abandonment of chronological time would be a leading feature in the great sacramental plays (*autos sacramentales*), best exemplified by Pedro Calderón de la Barca. The critics are in agreement too that Gil Vicente's work in religious drama in general was an important step forward in the history of that *genre*. "The first writer of Moralities [in the Peninsula]," wrote Alexander A. Parker, "is Gil Vicente in such plays as the *Auto da Alma*, the *Auto da História de Deus*, and more typically still in the trilogy of the *Barcas*." [11] Other countries in Europe possessed well developed morality plays before him, but it was left to Gil Vicente to take the first and significant step forward for Portugal and Spain.

"A long line of types drawn vividly from the various social strata pass through the whole of Vicente's extraordinary work," states João de Almeida Lucas;[12] and it is indeed true that the audience of the day, in the Portuguese Court, must have been intrigued to see, from play to play, a picturesque procession of contemporary types which they had seen in real life in the towns and in the countryside of their native land. The pastoral plays, the farces, the religious plays—in this great variety (a variety which the later Spanish *comedia* of Lope de Vega would imitate as a very special feature)—give us a fairly accurate picture of life of the day, in spite of the frequent poetic, allegorical clothing in which it is garbed. The Vicentine theater, it can be truly said, is in general terms a dramatic representation of Portuguese life in the first third of the sixteenth century.

III   Gil Vicente's Followers

It is a fact that, as Marcelino Menéndez Pelayo put it, "Gil Vicente's legitimate descendency was in Castile," [13] and it is an understatement on George Tyler Northup's part that "Lope de Vega was not above taking hints from him." [14] But in Portugal itself, it cannot be said that Gil Vicente was followed by any dramatist of outstanding ability. In spite of the fact that mention is sometimes made of a Vicentine "school," [15] the products of this so-called school are of little significance. The blame cannot be thrown upon Gil Vicente himself, but rather upon inept followers, changing tastes, and ecclesiastical censorship (which led the dramatists to prudence and subterfuge). Gil Vicente wrote, we remember, the slight *Play of St. Martin* very early in his career (his only "life of the saints"), but quickly turned his back on that *genre* to enter into other fields, more "dramatic," and preferred, it seems, by the Court audience. Among a more popular audience, however, the mediocre plays on the saints by one of Gil Vicente's "followers" seemed to have reached a certain vogue. Around the 1530's, Afonso Alvares, of Lisbon, wrote drama on St. Anthony, St. Barbara, St. James, and St. Vincent, in a style now "enriched," and far from that of the simple "master." One interesting reminiscence of the Vicentine manner is found in *The Play of St. Vincent (Auto de S. Vicente)* in Afonso Alvares' use of both Portuguese and Spanish. Another "popular" dramatist who devoted his efforts to the edification of the populace through the portrayal of the lives of the saints was the Madeiran Baltasar Dias. He presented on the stage St. Alexis and St. Catharine; adding a *Play on the Birth of Christ (Auto do Nascimento de Cristo)*. Writing in comrrect, monotonous verse, he is far from the spontaneous ease of the Vicentine lyrics.

António Ribeiro Chiado, a gay friar who died in Lisbon in 1591, wrote, in the middle of the sixteenth century, several plays inspired by his own experiences among the lower classes of that city. His *Conversation of the Cronies (Prática dos Compadres)* and his *Play of the Fishwives (Auto das Regateiras)*, for example, are little sketches of customs, slightly connected with Vicentine plays such as *Inês Pereira*. Of the same type is the anonymous *Play of Vicente Anes Joeira (Auto de Vicente Anes Joeira)*, which also presents types from Lisbon's lower classes. Likewise anonymous, with a Vicentine connection, is *The Play of the Day of Judgment* (*Auto do Dia do Juizo*), apparently modelled on the *Ships. The Play of Human Genesis* (*Obra da Geração Humana*) and *The Play of God the Father, Justice and Mercy* (*Auto de Deus Padre, Justiça e Misericórdia*), claimed unsuccessfully as Vicente's, are creditable pieces. Farce, in the Vicentine manner, had followers in Jerónimo Ribeiro's *Play of the Doctor* (*Auto do Físico*) and an António de Lisbona's *Play of the Two Thieves* (*Auto dos Dous Ladrões*).

The "classical" stream, completely opposed to the manner of Gil Vicente, which came into Portugal from Italy with Francisco de Sá de Miranda, after his sojourn there in the years 1521–1526, is of slight significance. It has no connection with Gil Vicente's "old fashioned," but live, medievalism, and only a couple of brighter stars like António Ferreira, with his tragedy *Castro,* and Jorge Ferreira de Vasconcelos, with his *Comédia Eufrosina,* redeem it in any way. Nor can much be said for several men who close the century, and who tried their hand at theater: the great epic poet, Luis de Camões, of a classical style, and António Prestes, Simão Machado, and Francisco da Costa, who are vaguely connected with the Vicentine vein. All of these dramatists who followed Gil Vicente in time only or in style have all but been lost in oblivion. Their theatrical poetry (or prose) is barren, their dramatic resources are slight; in short, they are but shadows in a century which has in drama one great name only, but one which is very great indeed!

"It seems a far cry from these simple plays [of Gil Vicente's] to the masterpieces of Shakespeare," wrote Bell on one occasion (*Gil Vicente,* p. 57). Yet Bell and others, including Ann Livermore in a perspicacious article,[16] would insist that Shakespeare may very well have been influenced directly or indirectly by Gil Vicente, and, as Bell puts it, "It is easier, with his plays in one's hand, to foretell the advent of a Lope de Vega, a Calderón, a Shakespeare, a Molière, than to foresee Vicente's best plays from the work of his predecessors or contemporaries, or his own early productions." Indeed, Agostinho de Campos would insist that Gil Vicente *was* a "precursor of Lope de Vega and of Molière" in a very real sense,[17] and critics in general agree that to our "great lyric poet and

charmingly incorrect playwright" the world of drama owes a great
deal. Gil Vicente's materials were old, but his treatment was re-
freshingly spontaneous and new. His stage instinct and his creative
imagination served him well and enabled him to produce a drama
which has led Aubrey F. G. Bell, his most fruitful critic, to say (*Gil
Vicente,* pp. 62–63) that in dialogue, he was "vivacious as Plautus,
in satire broad and reckless as Aristophanes, in portraiture piti-
lessly life-like as the author of *Lazarillo de Tormes,* in lyric poetry
an Elizabethan before Elizabeth, with the elusive charm of the
early Galician poetry, but with the concrete force of an artist and
the fervent ecstasy of a mystic." "Owing to his genius," concludes
Bell, "Portugal, with a literature essentially undramatic and lyrical, may claim a very important place in the history of the drama."

Notes and References

Preface

1. *Gil Vicente: Poeta* (Ponta Delgada: Author, 1963), p. 7.
2. *Gil Vicente e o teatro moderno (Tentativa de esquematização da obra vicentina)* (Lisbon: Minerva, 1965), p. 9.
3. A recent interesting note on the subject is that by Jack E. Tomlins, "Una nota sobre la clasificación de los dramas de Gil Vicente," *Duquesne Hispanic Review*, III (1964), 115–131; IV (1965), 1–16.
4. Luíza Maria de Castro e Azevedo, *Bibliografia vicentina* (Lisbon: Biblioteca Nacional, 1942).

Chapter One

1. The edition of Gil Vicente's Complete Works used and referred to in this study is the *Obras completas,* ed. Marques Braga, 6 vols., (Lisbon: Sá da Costa, 1942–1944). The *Auto da festa* is to be found in Vol. VI, pp. 131–169; and this quotation may be found on pp. 155–156.
2. *Gil Vicente: Guimarães, sua terra natal* (Guimarães: Author, 1959).
3. *Gil Vicente* (Marinha Grande: Empreza Typographica, 1894).
4. "Notas sôbre a linguagem de Gil Vicente," *Revista Lusitana* (Oporto), II (1891–1892), 340–343; and *Gil Vicente e a linguagem popular* (Lisbon: L. da Silva, 1902).
5. See Bibliography.
6. *Vida e obras de Gil Vicente "Trovador, mestre da Balança,"* 2nd ed. corrected (Lisbon: Revista Ocidente, 1944).
7. *Gil Vicente, beirão. Nasceu em Guimarães de Tavares* (Oporto: Casa da Beira Alta, 1966).
8. *Notas Vicentinas, IV: Cultura intelectual e nobreza literária* (Coimbra: Universidade de Coimbra, 1922), p. 234.
9. "Os sermões de Gil Vicente e a arte de pregar," in *Estudos sôbre a cultura portuguesa do século XVI,* Vol. II (Coimbra: Universidade de Coimbra, 1948), pp. 205–339.

10. *Les Sermons de Gil Vicente. En marge d'un opuscule du professeur Joaquim de Carvalho* (Lisbon: Ottosgráfica, 1949).

11. For example, in *Gil Vicente e as origens do teatro nacional* (Oporto: Chardron, 1898).

12. See his *História da cultura em Portugal,* Vol. II (Lisbon: Jornal do Fôro, 1955), p. 234, note 1.

13. Óscar de Pratt, in *Gil Vicente, Notas e comentários* (Lisbon: Teixeira, 1931), p. 266, states rightly (but not to argue the question) that "the mechanical arts . . . appear rarely in the Vicentine plays."

14. *Four Plays of Gil Vicente.* Edited from the *editio princeps* (1562), with translation and notes, by Aubrey F. G. Bell (Cambridge, England: Cambridge University, 1920), p. xii.

15. Aubrey F. G. Bell, *Gil Vicente* (Oxford: Oxford University, 1921), p. 3.

16. "Fixação da data da celebração vicentina," in *Gil Vicente: Vida e obra* (Série de conferências realizadas na Academia das Ciências de Lisboa, de 8 de abril a 21 de junho de 1937, em comemoração do IV Centenário do fundador do teatro português) (Lisbon: Academia das Ciências, 1939), pp. 19–24. The quotation is on p. 24.

17. Aubrey F. G. Bell, *Lyrics of Gil Vicente,* 2nd ed. (Oxford: Blackwell, 1921), p. 37.

18. In 1834, in Hamburg, published by Langhoff, appeared the *Obras de Gil Vicente,* in 3 vols., edited by J. V. Barreto and J. G. Monteiro.

19. "La Censure inquisitoriale et les oeuvres de Gil Vicente," *Bulletin d'Histoire du Théâtre Portugais* (Lisbon), I (1950), 117–119.

20. "El verdadero texto de la *Copilação* vicentina de 1562," in *Studia Philologica: Homenaje ofrecido a Dámaso Alonso,* III (Madrid: Gredos, 1963), pp. 55–68. Another copy, which I saw in the Biblioteca Nacional, Madrid, in the summer of 1966, has quite a few folios missing.

21. I. S. Révah discusses certain reservations he has about Luis Vicente's editorial procedures in his *Édition critique du premier Auto das Barcas* (Lisbon: Centre d'Histoire du Théâtre Portugais, 1951), and in his *Édition critique de l'Auto de Inês Pereira* (Lisbon: Centre d'Histoire du Théâtre Portugais, 1955); these two plays having appeared separately in presumably earlier and more accurate versions.

22. *Deux autos méconnus de Gil Vicente. Première édition moderne* (Lisbon: Ottosgráfica, 1948), and *Deux autos de Gil Vicente restitués à leur auteur* (Lisbon: Academia das Ciências, 1949).

23. In discussions of Révah's theses in *Biblos* (Coimbra), XXIV (1948), 571–574, and XXV (1949), 439–444.

Notes and References

24. *La Langue de Gil Vicente* (Paris: Klinsksieck, 1959), pp. 8–12.

25. A good account of the discussions of this lost play, which was listed on the Portuguese *Index* of 1551, is to be found in an article by I. S. Révah: "L'Attribution du *Jubilé d'Amour* à Gil Vicente," *Bulletin des Études Portugaises et de L'Institut Français au Portugal,* nouvelle série, XII (1948), 273–278; and in a "note" by Carolina Michaëlis de Vasconcelos: "Gil Vicente em Bruxelas ou o *Jubileu de Amor,*" *Notas Vicentinas,* I (Coimbra: Universidade de Coimbra, 1912), 9–83.

26. See Teyssier, pp. 298–301. Also worthy of note is Albin Eduard Beau's "Sobre el bilingüismo en Gil Vicente," in *Studia Philologica: Homenaje ofrecido a Dámaso Alonso,* I (Madrid: Gredos, 1960), pp. 217–224.

27. *A History of Portugal* (Cambridge, England: Cambridge University, 1947), pp. 238–239.

28. See J. H. Parker, "Gil Vicente: A Study in Peninsular Drama," *Hispania,* XXXVI (1953), 21–25.

29. See I. S. Révah, "Gil Vicente a-t-il été le fondateur du théâtre portugais?" *Bulletin d'Histoire du Théâtre Portugais,* I (1950), 153–185.

30. *Itinerario del entremés desde Lope de Rueda a Quiñones de Benavente* (Madrid: Gredos, 1965), p. 37.

31. This letter, which is preserved in the Archives of Simancas, Spain, has been reproduced by I. S. Révah in his article on "Manifestations théatrales pré-vincentines: Les *momos* de 1500," *Bulletin d'Histoire du Théâtre Portugais,* III (1952), 91–105.

32. *Storia del teatro portoghese* (Rome: Ateneo, 1964), p. 57.

33. "Ébauches dramatiques dans le *Cancioneiro Geral,*" *Bulletin d'Histoire du Théâtre Portugais,* II (1951), 113–150.

34. "La *Comedia* dans l'oeuvre de Gil Vicente," *Bulletin d'Histoire du Théâtre Portugais,* II (1951), 1–39.

Chapter Two

1. See Charlotte Stern, "*Sayago* and *sayagués* in Spanish History and Literature," *Hispanic Review,* XXIX (1961), 217–237; and Dámaso Alonso, "Problemas del castellano vicentino," in his edition of *Don Duardos,* Vol. II (Madrid: Consejo Superior de Investigaciones Científicas, 1942), pp. 117–154.

2. *Introito and Loa in the Spanish Drama of the Sixteenth Century* (Philadelphia: University of Pennsylvania, 1928), p. 10. (University of Pennsylvania Series in Romanic Languages and Literatures, No. 16.)

3. *The Staging of Plays in the Spanish Peninsula Prior to 1555*

(Iowa City: University of Iowa, 1935), p. 30. (University of Iowa Studies in Spanish Language and Literature, No. 5.)

4. *Introducción al teatro religioso del Siglo de Oro* (Madrid: Revista de Occidente, 1953), p. 164.

5. "Lucas Fernández and the Evolution of the Shepherd's Family Pride in Early Spanish Drama," *Hispanic Review,* XXV (1957), 252–263. Quotation, p. 256.

6. In the *Obras dramáticas castellanas* (Madrid: Espasa-Calpe, 1962), pp. 35–36.

7. For a recent and penetrating study of Mendoza's *Vita Christi,* see Charlotte Stern, "Fray Iñigo de Mendoza and Medieval Dramatic Ritual," *Hispanic Review,* XXXIII (1965), 197–245.

8. *The Court Theatre of Gil Vicente* (Lisbon: Author, 1962), p. 118.

9. Eduardo González Pedroso used the *Auto de S. Martinho* to head his collection of *Autos sacramentales,* in *Biblioteca de Autores Españoles,* LVIII (Madrid: Rivadeneyra, 1865), although admitting that the piece had no connection with the institution of the Eucharist. Nicolás González Ruiz included the play in his *Piezas maestras del teatro teológico español,* Vol. I (Madrid: Biblioteca de Autores Cristianos, 1946), and while rejecting *S. Martinho* specifically as an *auto sacramental,* he still accepted its date—1504—as the year of birth of the *genre.*

10. "*Comedias, tragicomedias* and *farsas* in Gil Vicente," in *Miscelânea de Filologia, Literatura e História Cultural à Memória de Francisco Adolfo Coelho (1847–1919),* Vol. II (Lisbon: Centro de Estudos Filológicos, 1950), pp. 268–280. Quotation, p. 279.

11. "*L'Auto de la Sibylle Cassandre* de Gil Vicente," *Hispanic Review,* XXVII (1959), 167–193. Quotation, p. 170.

12. "Approaching the Metaphysical Sense of Gil Vicente's Chivalric Tragicomedies," *Bulletin of the Comediantes,* XVI, 1 (Spring, 1964), 1–9. Quotations, pp. 3–4.

13. "El *Auto dos Quatro Tempos* de Gil Vicente," *Revista de Filología Española,* XXXIII (1949), 350–375. Quotation, p. 350.

Chapter Three

1. *The Play of the Sibyl Cassandra* (Bryn Mawr: Bryn Mawr College 1921).

2. "Gil Vicente's *Auto de la sibila Casandra,*" *Hispanic Review,* XXVI (1958), 35–51.

3. "Para la génesis del *Auto de la Sibila Casandra,*" *Filología* (Buenos Aires), V (1959), 47–63.

4. "The Artistic Unity of Gil Vicente's *Auto da Sibila Cassandra*," *Hispanic Review*, XXVII (1959), 56–77.

5. See Chapter Two, note 11.

6. *The Limits of Literary Criticism* (London: Oxford University Press, 1956), p. 39.

7. *Spanish Drama Before Lope de Vega*, revised edition (Philadelphia: University of Pennsylvania, 1937), p. 36.

8. "The Songs of Gil Vicente," *Atlante* (London), I (1953), 3–21. (Reprinted in *Inspiration and Poetry*, London: Macmillan, 1955, pp. 90–111.)

9. See his edition of *Poesías de Gil Vicente* (Mexico: Séneca, 1940). Earlier published in *Cruz y Raya*, No. 10 (1934), pp. 1–46.

10. *History of Spanish Literature*, Vol. I (New York: Harper, 1849), p. 286.

11. For the *mise en scène*, including the use of a backstage, see Williams, *The Staging of Plays* (referred to in Chapter Two, note 3) and William H. Shoemaker, *The Multiple Stage in Spain during the Fifteenth and Sixteenth Centuries* (Princeton: Princeton University, 1935), pp. 95, 100–101 [which was translated into Spanish as *Los escenarios mútiples en el teatro español de los siglos XV y XVI* (Barcelona: Instituto del Teatro, 1957)].

12. In his small anthology, *Teatro de Gil Vicente* (Lisbon: Portugália, 1959), p. 57.

13. *La Pastorale. Essai d'analyse littéraire* (Assen: Van Goscum, 1950), p. 141.

14. See Chapter Two, note 13.

15. For a study of the poem, see Inez Macdonald, "The *Coronación* of Juan de Mena: Poem and Commentary," *Hispanic Review*, VII (1939), 125–144.

16. For a description of the treatise, see Lynn Thorndike, *A History of Magic and Experimental Science*, Vol. II (New York: Columbia University, 1947), 401–435.

Chapter Four

1. *Notas Vicentinas, II: A rainha velha e o Monólogo do Vaqueiro* (Coimbra: Universidade de Coimbra, 1918), p. 11.

2. The Portuguese text is to be found in *Obras completas*, II, 39–82; and an English verse translation in *Gil Vicente, The Ship of Hell*, by A. F. Gerald [Bell] (Watford, England: Voss, 1929), pp. 16–43.

3. For example, by Paulo Quintela (Coimbra: Universidade de Coimbra, 1946), Charles David Ley (Madrid: Aguirre, 1946), and by I. S. Révah (Madrid: Centre d'Histoire du Théâtre Portugais, 1951).

4. The Portuguese text is in *Obras completas*, II, 83–123; and an English verse translation in *The Ship of Hell*, pp. 45–70.

5. The Portuguese text is in *Obras completas*, II, 125–169; and an English verse translation in *The Ship of Hell*, pp. 71–98.

6. The Portuguese text is in *Obras completas*, II, 1–37; and this text, with an English verse translation, is in Bell's *Four Plays of Gil Vicente*, pp. 1–21.

7. "Las fuentes de las *Barcas* de Gil Vicente. Lógica intelectual e imaginación dramática," *Bulletin d'Histoire du Théâtre Portugais*, IV (1953), 207–237.

8. "La Source de la *Obra da Geração humana* et de l'*Auto da Alma*," *Bulletin d'Histoire du Théâtre Portugais*, I (1950), 1–32.

9. *Storia della letteratura portoghese* (Florence: Sansoni, 1953), p. 54.

10. *História do teatro português no século XVI* (Oporto: Imprensa Portugueza, 1870), pp. 104–105.

11. See *Vita Christi*, trans. by Ambrosio Montesino, Alcalá de Henares, 1502, fol. cxvi, col. a.

12. Joaquim Pedro Oliveira Martins, *Camões, Os Lusíadas, e a Renascença em Portugal* (Oporto: Chardron, 1891), p. 135.

13. *O Judeu em Gil Vicente* (São Paulo: Conselho Estadual de Cultura, 1963), pp. 40–48.

14. *Gil Vicente e o fim do teatro medieval* (Lisbon: Europa-América, 1942), p. 68.

15. "L'*Auto de la Cananéenne* de Gil Vicente et sa place dans l'année liturgique," *Bulletin d'Études Portugaises et de l'Institut Français au Portugal*, XII (1948), 265–272.

16. "La *Cananeia* de Gil Vicente et les mystères français," *Bulletin Hispanique*, L (1948), 353–369.

Chapter Five

1. For example, by Maximiano Lemos, *O Auto dos Físicos de Gil Vicente: Comentário médico* (Oporto: Enciclopedia Portuguesa, 1921); A. da Rocha Brito, "A Farsa dos Físicos de Gil Vicente vista por um médico," *Biblos* (Coimbra), XII (1936), 336–420; and by Egas Moniz, "Os médicos no teatro vicentino," in *Gil Vicente: Vida e obra* (Academia das Ciências de Lisboa, 1939), pp. 49–90.

2. See Mrs. Stern's review of the Alonso Zamora Vicente edition of the *Comedia del Viudo* (Lisbon: Centro de Estudos Filológicos, 1962), in *Hispanic Review*, XXXI (1963), 359–362.

3. *Tragicomedia de Amadís de Gaula*, ed. T. P. Waldron (Manchester, England: Manchester University, 1959), p. 14, note 2.

Notes and References

4. To be found in his article "La *Comedia* dans l'oeuvre de Gil Vicente" (see Chapter One, note 34), pp. 24–25.

5. "Some Relations of Bibliography to Editorial Problems," in *Studies in Bibliography* (Papers of the Bibliographical Society, University of Virginia, Charlottesville), III (1950–1951), p. 52.

6. See, for example, Jacob Ornstein's "La misoginia y el pro-femenismo en la literature castellana," *Revista de Filología Hispánica*, III (1941), 219–232.

7. *The Approach to the Spanish Drama of the Golden Age* (London: The Hispanic and Luso-Brazilian Councils, 1957), p. 14.

8. Good studies of this question are Marcel Bataillon, *Erasmo y España*, II (Mexico-Buenos Aires: Fondo de Cultura Económica, 1950); and João R. Mendes, "Do erasmismo de Gil Vicente," *Brotéria*, XXIII (1936), 303–319.

9. *Édition Critique de l'"Auto de Inês Pereira"* (Lisbon: Centre d'Histoire du Théâtre Portugais, 1955). [Previously printed in *Bulletin d'Histoire du Théâtre Portugais*, III–IV (1952–1954).]

10. "A mulher na obra de Gil Vicente," in *Gil Vicente: Vida e obra* (Academia das Ciências de Lisboa, 1939), pp. 411–469.

11. "Gil Vicente e os homens do fôro," in *Gil Vicente: Vida e obra* (Academia das Ciências de Lisboa, 1939), pp. 205–255.

12. "Gil Vicente e a reforma," in *Gil Vicente: Vida e obra* (Academia das Ciências de Lisboa, 1939), pp. 383–409.

13. *The Waning of the Middle Ages* (Garden City, New York: Doubleday, 1954), p. 178. (First published in 1924.)

14. "Juan del Encina's Carnival Eclogues and the Spanish Drama of the Renaissance," *Renaissance Drama*, VIII (1965), 181–195.

Chapter Six

1. See I. S. Révah, "La *Comedia* dans l'oeuvre de Gil Vicente," pp. 10–12 (Chapter One, note 34).

2. See Chapter Five, note 3.

3. Madrid, Consejo Superior de Investigaciones Científicas, 1942.

4. See Elza Fernandes Paxeco, "Da *Tragicomédia de Dom Duardos*," *Revista da Faculdade de Letras da Universidade de Lisboa*, V (1938), 193–203.

5. Dámaso Alonso, in "El hidalgo Camilote y el hidalgo don Quijote," *Revista de Filología Española*, XX (1933), 391–397, XXI (1934), 283–284, suggests that this part of *Dom Duardos* may have inspired Cervantes' Don Quixote-Dulcinea situation of a similar nature.

6. See my review of the Waldron edition of *Amadis de Gaula*, in *Hispania*, XLIV (1961), 197–198.

7. "Approaching the Metaphysical Sense of Gil Vicente's Chivalric Tragicomedies." See Chapter Two, note 12. The quotation is on p. 7.

8. "Courtly Love in Gil Vicente's *Don Duardos*," *Romance Notes*, II (1960–1961), 103–106.

9. "The Unity of *Don Duardos*," *Modern Language Notes*, LXXVI (1961), 759–766.

Chapter Seven

1. "Une source de Gil Vicente et de Montemor: La Méditation de Savonarole sur le *Miserere*," in *Études sur le Portugal au Temps de l'Humanisme*, Acta Universitatis Conimbrigensis (Coimbra, 1952), pp. 197–217.

2. "Notas Vicentinas. IV" (Chapter One, note 8), p. 96.

3. "Notas Vicentinas. III: Romance à morte del Rei Dom Manuel e à Aclamação de Dom João Terceiro" (Coimbra: Universidade de Coimbra, 1919).

4. Gil Vicente's lines may be found in the facsimile edition of the *Cancioneiro Geral* (New York, De Vinne, 1904), fol. CCX^{vo}.

5. The short epitaph, which is the final item in the *Copilação*, has already been referred to in Chapter One. (One other brief paragraph attributed to Gil Vicente is the prologue-dedication to João III of the play *Dom Duardos* in the 1586 *Copilação*. This does not appear in the first printing of the *Copilação* of 1562.)

6. Naples: Istituto Universitario Orientale, 1963.

7. *História da cultura em Portugal*, II (Chapter One, note 12), p. 270.

Chapter Eight

1. "Canto, dança e música nos Autos de Gil Vicente," pp. 499–516. Mention has already been made of Bell's *Lyrics of Gil Vicente* (Chapter One, note 17), Bowra's "The Songs of Gil Vicente" (Chapter Three, note 8), and Dámaso Alonso's *Poesías de Gil Vicente* (Chapter Three, note 9). Joaquim Mendes dos Remédios in *Obras de Gil Vicente*, Vol. III (Coimbra: França Amado, 1914), devoted a section (pp. 263–293) to "Versos líricos ou Fragmentos de canções dispersos nas Obras de Gil Vicente." Agostinho de Campos wrote on "O elemento lírico nos autos de Gil Vicente" in *Gil Vicente: Vida e obra* (Academia das Ciências de Lisboa, 1939), pp. 123–157. Other studies of value are Pierre LeGentil's "Notes sur les compositions lyriques du théâtre de Gil Vicente," in *Mélanges d'Histoire du Théâtre du Moyen-Âge et de la Renaissance offerts à Gustave Cohen* (Paris: Nizet, 1950), pp. 249–260; Eugenio Asensio's "Gil Vicente y las cantigas paralelísticas 'restauradas'. ¿Folklore o poesía original?", in *Poética y*

realidad en el Cancionero peninsular de la Edad Media (Madrid: Gredos, 1957), pp. 133–180 (Gil Vicente's use of songs and music), and Albin Eduard Beau's "A música na obra de Gil Vicente," in *Estudos,* I (Coimbra: Universidade de Coimbra, 1959), pp. 219–249. A very recent volume, partly dealing with songs, is Thomas R. Hart's *Gil Vicente: Poesía* (Salamanca: Anaya, 1965).

2. *Portugal: An Anthology* (Oxford: Clarendon Press, 1916), p. 57.

3. *Comparative Literature,* XVII (1965), 225–233.

Chapter Nine

1. *Um Auto de Gil Vicente,* ed. J. W. Barker (London: Sidgwick & Jackson, 1935), pp. 43–44. This edition also contains the text of Gil Vicente's *Cortes de Jupiter.*

2. *Portuguese Literature* (Oxford: Oxford University, 1922), p. 133.

3. "Ida da Infanta Dona Beatriz pera Saboya," in *Chronica del Rey Dom João II* (Lisbon, 1752), fol. 99 v.

4. *A History of Portugal* (New York: D. van Nostrand, 1952), p. 113.

Chapter Ten

1. "Gil Vicente, poeta cómico," *Bulletin d'Histoire du Théâtre Portugais,* II (1951), 181–211. (This quotation is on p. 201.)

2. See Chapter Four, note 14: *Gil Vicente e o fim do teatro medieval,* p. 129 passim.

3. See Chapter One, note 12: *História da cultura em Portugal,* II, 231.

4. "Gil Vicente: O aspecto 'medieval' e 'renascentista' da sua obra," in *Estudos,* I (Coimbra: Universidade de Coimbra, 1959), pp. 73–158 [previously published in *Boletim de Filologia,* IV, V (1936, 1937–1938)].

5. "If humanism is essentially the interest in what is human, Gil Vicente is a humanist"—Hernâni Cidade, *Lições de cultura luso-brasileira* (Rio de Janeiro: Livros de Portugal, 1960), p. 116.

6. See Chapter Five, note 14: "Juan del Encina's Carnival Eclogues. . . ."

7. "Gil Vicente et la théorie de l'art dramatique," in *Études dédiées à Andreas Blinkenberg* (Copenhagen: Munksgaard, 1963), pp. 209–219.

8. J. Richard Andrews, in "The Harmonizing Perspective of Gil Vicente," *Bulletin of the Comediantes,* XI, No. 2 (Fall, 1959), 1–5, would object that many of the modern critics' charges against the Vicentine theater are "invalid," in that Gil Vicente "places a preferential value on harmony," striving "to see concord where a dramatist

would have emphasized strife," in his process of "creating a theater as lyrical analogue."

9. "A linguagem anatómica de Gil Vicente," *Biblos*, XII (1936), 529–572. (This quotation is on p. 572.)

10. In the stage directions of the *Copilação*, we read (*Obras completas*, V, 72): "Here the girl speaks to him from the window in such a low voice that no one hears her, and by the words which he answers one can guess what she says to him" ("Aqui lhe fala a moça da janela tam passo que ninguem a ouve, e polas palabras que elle responde se póde conjeturar o que lhe ella diz").

11. "Notes on the Religious Drama in Medieval Spain and the Origins of the *Auto sacramental*," *Modern Language Review*, XXX (1935), 170–182. (This quotation is on p. 179.)

12. In his edition of *O Velho da Horta* [*The Old Man of the Orchard*] (Lisbon: Império, 1943), p. 8.

13. *Antología de poetas líricos castellanos desde la formación del idioma hasta nuestros días*, VII (Madrid: Hernando, 1898), p. ccxix.

14. *An Introduction to Spanish Literature*, 3rd ed., revised by Nicholson B. Adams (Chicago: University of Chicago, 1960), p. 239.

15. See, for example, Teófilo Braga, *Escola de Gil Vicente e desenvolvimento do teatro nacional* (*História da literatura portuguesa*), Vol. VIIIa (Oporto: Chardron, 1898); Carolina Michaëlis de Vasconcelos (ed.), *Autos portugueses de Gil Vicente y de la escuela vicentina* (Madrid: Centro de Estudios Históricos, 1922); and Gustavo de Matos Sequeira, "Os continuadores de Gil Vicente," in *História da literatura portuguesa*, ed. Albino Forjaz de Sampaio, Vol. II (Paris-Lisbon, Aillaud & Bertrand, 1929), pp. 97–139.

16. "Gil Vicente e Shakespeare," *Revista da Faculdade de Letras*, Universidade de Lisboa, XVII (1951), 140–149.

17. "Gil Vicente: Un précurseur de Lope de Vega et de Molière," *Biblos*, XII (1936), 421–435.

Selected Bibliography

Useful Printings of Gil Vicente's Works

Obras completas. Edited by Marques Braga. 6 vols. (Lisbon: Sá da Costa, 1942–1944.) [Later printings.] This very good edition contains a useful introduction and valuable notes. It follows the order of the *Copilação* of 1562.

Obras dramáticas castellanas. Edited by Thomas R. Hart. (Madrid: Espasa-Calpe, 1962.) (Clásicos Castellanos, 156.) An excellent compilation of the plays in Spanish, with introduction and notes.

Four Plays of Gil Vicente. Edited by Aubrey F. G. Bell. (Cambridge, England: Cambridge University, 1920.) This edition has been made from the *editio princeps* (1562). There is a splendid introduction on the dramatist's life and works, copious notes, and the original text, with English verse translation of four plays: *The Soul's Journey, Exhortation to War, The Farce of the Carriers,* and *The Pastoral Tragicomedy of the Estrêla Mountain Range.*

The Ship of Hell by Gil Vicente. English version by A. F. Gerald [Bell]. (Watford, England: Voss, 1929.) An excellent edition, comprising an introduction and English verse translations of *The Ship of Hell, The Ship of Purgatory,* and *The Ship of Heaven.*

Lyrics of Gil Vicente. Edited by Aubrey F. G. Bell. (2nd ed.) (Oxford: Blackwell, 1921.) Fifty-one lyrics, chiefly from the plays, are presented with the Portuguese, or Spanish, original text and English verse translations. Invaluable.

Poesías de Gil Vicente. Edited by Dámaso Alonso. (Mexico: Séneca, 1940.) (Earlier published in the Spanish periodical, *Cruz y Raya,* No. 10, 1934, pp. 1–46.) Dámaso Alonso has carefully chosen and skilfully edited Gil Vicente's Spanish "songs" which are found in his plays.

Tragicomedia de Amadís de Gaula. Edited by T. P. Waldron. (Manchester, England: Manchester University, 1959.) A fine edition, with a good introduction, text, and notes.

Tragicomedia de Don Duardos. Edited by Dámaso Alonso. (Madrid: Consejo Superior de Investigaciones Científicas, 1942.) In addition to presenting the text, there is a good study of the dramatic poetry in the play and of the problems relating to Gil Vicente's Spanish.

Comedia del viudo. Edited by Alonso Zamora Vicente. (Lisbon: Centro de Estudos Filológicos, 1962.) A good edition of one of Gil Vicente's farces, and a good example of recent printings of the dramatist's individual plays.

Il Pranto de Maria Parda. Edited by Luciana Stegagno Picchio. (Naples: Istituto Universitario Orientale, 1963.) A scholarly edition of the Harvard University copy of this non-dramatic work.

Useful Works of Criticism

Academia das Ciências de Lisboa. *Gil Vicente: Vida e obra*. (Lisbon: Academia das Ciências, 1939.) A series of lectures of significance, dealing with topics such as the physician in the plays, lyricism in the plays, Gil Vicente's presentation of law, religious reform, and his views on women.

Bell, Aubrey F. G. *Gil Vicente*. (Oxford: Oxford University, 1921.) A short, but basic account of Gil Vicente's life and works by the most important of Vicentine scholars.

Braamcamp Freire, Anselmo. *Vida e obras de Gil Vicente "Trovador, mestre da Balança."* 2nd ed. corrected. (Lisbon: Revista Ocidente, 1944.) The standard detailed study of Gil Vicente's life and works. Indispensable for a knowledge of the dramatist, and most highly recommended.

Braga, Teófilo. *Gil Vicente e as origens do teatro nacional*. (Oporto: Chardron, 1898.) (*História da literatura portuguesa*. Vol. VIII.) An old-fashioned but basically sound general study of the beginning of the Portuguese theater by the leading Portuguese historian of literature at the turn of the present century.

Castro e Azevedo, Luíza Maria de. *Bibliografia vicentina*. (Lisbon: Biblioteca Nacional, 1942.) This large volume, published by the Biblioteca Nacional, Lisbon, is a most valuable tool for Vicentine scholarship.

Keates, Laurence. *The Court Theatre of Gil Vicente*. (Lisbon: Author, 1962.) A rather superficial but valiant attempt to present Gil Vicente the Court Impresario.

Láfer, Celso. *O Judeu em Gil Vicente*. (São Paulo: Conselho Estadual de Cultura, 1963.) A monograph which gives valuable insight into Gil Vicente's presentation of the society of his day and especially the "New Christian."

Pratt, Oscar de. *Gil Vicente: Notas e comentários*. (Lisbon: Teixeira,

1931.) Contains useful "notes and commentaries" of very diversified aspects of Gil Vicente the man and his works.

Révah, I. S. "Gil Vicente a-t-il été le fondateur du théâtre portugais?" *Bulletin d'Histoire du Théâtre Portugais*, I (1950), 153–185. A penetrating investigation of the question: in what sense may Gil Vicente be looked upon as the "founder" of the Portuguese theater?

Saraiva, António José. *Gil Vicente e o fim do teatro medieval.* (Lisbon: Europa-América, 1942.) Gil Vicente is set in the history of theater as a man with whom the Middle Ages comes to an end. Saraiva later modified his opinion to glimpse certain Renaissance aspects in the dramatist, but the first thesis is the correct one.

Teyssier, Paul. *La Langue de Gil Vicente.* (Paris: Klinsksieck, 1959.) Gil Vicente's fascinating bilingualism (Portuguese and Spanish) is satisfactorily explained in this careful study of the subject.

Vasconcelos, Carolina Michaëlis de. *Notas Vicentinas.* I-IV. (Coimbra: Universidade de Coimbra, 1912–1922.) Not even a "selected bibliography" would be complete without paying tribute to the indefatigable work on behalf of Vicentine scholarship by this outstanding critic. The "Notes" discuss wide aspects of his life and works.

Valuable Background Materials

Bell, Aubrey F. G. *Portuguese Literature.* (Oxford: Oxford University, 1922.) The standard and basic history of Portuguese literature, in which Gil Vicente is well treated.

Crawford, J. P. Wickersham. *Spanish Drama before Lope de Vega.* Revised edition. (Philadelphia: University of Pennsylvania, 1937.) A time-tested study of Gil Vicente, his Spanish predecessors, contemporaries and followers.

Livermore, Harold V. *A History of Portugal.* (Cambridge, England: Cambridge University, 1947.) Useful for the background of the Vicentine theater. [A revised *New History of Portugal* has appeared in 1966.]

Nowell, Charles E. *A History of Portugal.* (New York: D. van Nostrand, 1952.) Likewise contains valuable discussions of Portugal during Vicente's lifetime.

Picchio, Luciana Stegagno. *Storia del teatro portoghese.* (Rome: Ateneo, 1964.) Gil Vicente and other Portuguese dramatists of the sixteenth century are fully treated.

Saraiva, António José. *História da cultura em Portugal.* Vol. II. (Lisbon: Jornal do Fôro, 1955.) Contains a splendid account of Gil

Vicente's activities at the Portuguese Court against the cultural background of the day.

Shoemaker, William H. *The Multiple Stage in Spain during the Fifteenth and Sixteenth Centuries.* (Princeton: Princeton University, 1935.) In Spanish translation: *Los escenarios múltiples en el teatro español en los siglos XV y XVI.* (Barcelona: Instituto del Teatro, 1957.) Although most attention is paid to Spain, the state of the Peninsular stage in general is sufficiently well described to explain Gil Vicente's simple procedures.

Wardropper, Bruce W. *Introducción al teatro religioso del Siglo de Oro.* (Madrid: Revista de Occidente, 1953.) Gil Vicente is presented as an essential link in the development of the Peninsular religious theater.

Williams, Ronald B. *The Staging of Plays in the Spanish Peninsula Prior to 1555.* (Iowa City: University of Iowa, 1935. University of Iowa Studies in Spanish Language and Literature, No. 5.) Careful attention is given to Gil Vicente's stage presentations at the Portuguese Court, and specific reference to individual plays is made.

Index

Afonso Henriques, King, 17, 78, 128
Alba, Duke of, 28, 31, 51, 97, 145
Almeida Garrett, 101, 133
Almeida Lucas, João de, 79, 80, 147
Almeida Pavão, José, 7
Alonso, Dámaso, 43, 44, 45, 100, 101, 104, 105, 123, 125, 127, 128, 129
Alvares, Afonso, 148
Aristophanes, 88, 125, 150
Asensio, Eugenio, 26, 35, 51, 52, 57, 58, 59, 147
Atkinson, William C., 34, 35
Auerbach, Erich, 43

Barberino, Andrea da, 38
Bartolomaeus Anglicus, 51
Bataillon, Marcel, 94, 95, 108, 109
Beatriz, Princess, 20, 75, 76, 77, 111, 127, 133, 134, 142
Beau, Albin Eduard, 122, 143, 144, 145
Bell, Aubrey Fitz Gerald, 17, 18, 19, 21, 29, 38, 43, 44, 45, 46, 47, 49, 50, 52, 54, 55, 56, 65, 66, 74, 75, 78, 84, 89, 90, 91, 93, 95, 98, 101, 118, 122, 123, 124, 125, 127, 128, 129, 130, 131, 134, 142, 143, 147, 149, 150
Bezerra, Branca, 21, 81
Book of Hours, The, 141
Bowers, Fredson, 80
Bowra, Cecil M., 43, 46, 123, 125, 126
Bowring, John, 130
Braamcamp Freire, Anselmo, 8, 17, 18, 19, 55, 73, 76, 99, 117, 121, 122, 135
Braga, Teófilo, 18, 59
Browning, Robert, 45

Cabral, Pedro Alvares, 20
Calderón de la Barca, Pedro, 147, 149
Camões, Luis de, 149
Campos, Agostinho de, 71, 72, 149
Carlos V, Emperor, 25, 88, 91, 99, 112, 128, 142
Carvalho, António Lopes de, 17
Carvalho, Joaquim de, 18
Catarina, Queen, 22, 23, 25, 66, 91, 95, 113, 114, 142
Catholic Sovereigns (Fernando and Isabel), 25, 26
Cavalcanti, Guido, 126
Celestina, The, 64, 78, 79, 87
Cervantes, Miguel de, 105, 119
Costa, Francisco da, 149
Costa Pimpão, Alvaro Júlio da, 23
Crawford, J. P. W., 43
Crónica Troyana, 39
Cunha, Tristão da, 47
Cunha Gonçalves, Luiz da, 89

Dance of Death, The, 58
Daniel, The Book of, 51
Dantas, Júlio, 22, 92
Dante, 58
David, Pierre, 71, 72
Day of Judgment, The Play of the, 149
Dias, Baltasar, 148

[165]

Duarte, Prince, 59

Encina, Juan del, 24, 26, 28, 30, 31, 32, 33, 34, 35, 36, 37, 51, 62, 68, 84, 97, 108, 123, 145
Erasmus, 52, 63, 85, 94, 95
Everyman, 54

Felipe, Prince, 97, 142
Fernández, Lucas, 24, 28, 30, 31, 32, 33, 34, 35, 36, 37, 55, 145
Fernández de Villegas, Pedro, 58, 59
Ferreira, António, 149
Ferreira de Vasconcelos, Jorge, 149
Fitzmaurice-Kelly, James, 43, 44

Gama, Vasco da, 19, 29
Gardner, Helen, 41
Gerhardt, Mia I., 49
God the Father, Justice and Mercy, The Play of, 23, 24, 149
Gower, John, 84

Hart, Thomas R., 33, 38, 39, 40, 41, 42, 45, 46, 81, 104, 106, 123, 140
Henry VIII, 20
Henry the Navigator, 20, 117
Hita, Arcipreste de, 125, 126
Horace, 79
Huizinga, Johan, 95, 145
Human Genesis, 23, 24, 149

Index of Prohibited Books, 22, 23, 52, 84
Inquisition, 22
Irving, Washington, 90
Isabel, Princess (Daughter of the Catholic Sovereigns), 19, 25
Isabel, Princess (Daughter of João III), 77, 142
Isabel, Princess (Sister of João III), 25, 75, 88, 99, 112, 128

João II, 19, 20, 134
João III, 20, 21, 22, 24, 25, 30, 32, 52, 65, 66, 75, 78, 81, 85, 87, 99,

112, 113, 114, 115, 116, 117, 120, 128, 134, 142
Job, The Book of, 62, 63, 67
Johnson, Harvey L., 129, 131

Keates, Laurence, 34, 54, 63, 64, 65, 66, 68, 69, 75, 76, 97, 134, 135
King, Georgiana Goddard, 38, 39, 140, 141

Láfer, Celso, 64, 69, 86
Lazarillo de Tormes, 150
Le Gentil, Georges, 72, 123
Leanor, Dowager Queen, 18, 19, 31, 34, 37, 55, 65, 109, 119, 141
Leanor, Queen (Wife of Manuel I), 25, 55, 83, 111, 112, 142
Leitão, Joaquim, 87
Leite de Vasconcelos, José, 17
Leo X, Pope, 20
Lida de Malkiel, María Rosa, 38, 39, 40, 41, 140, 141
Lihani, John, 32
Lisbona, António de, 149
Livermore, Ann, 149
Livermore, Harold V., 25
Longfellow, Henry Wadsworth, 111, 129, 130, 131
Lucian of Samosata, 58, 94
Ludolphus de Saxonia, 33, 59, 60, 61
Luis, Prince, 109, 110, 113
Luke, The Book of, 60
Luther, Martin, 24, 95

Machado, Simão, 149
Manrique, Jorge, 52, 54, 80, 111
Manrique, Rodrigo, 81, 111
Manuel, Prince, 24, 96
Manuel I, 19, 20, 21, 25, 26, 29, 30, 36, 47, 55, 75, 83, 93, 99, 109, 111, 112, 120, 133, 134
Maria, Princess, 93, 135
Maria, Queen, 25, 29, 30, 55, 75, 142
Mark, The Book of, 70
Marques, Amândio, 18
Marques Braga, 63, 78, 141, 143
Matthew, The Book of, 40, 70, 71

Index

Mena, Juan de, 51
Mendes dos Remédios, Joaquim, 123
Mendoza, Fray Iñigo de, 33
Menéndez Pelayo, Marcelino, 46, 101, 148
Meredith, Joseph A., 30, 34
Michaëlis de Vasconcelos, Carolina, 18, 54, 109, 113, 135
Molière, 79, 146, 149
Montalvo, 102
Montesino, Fray Ambrosio, 33, 81
Mota, Anrique da, 26, 27, 118, 119, 120, 121

Northup, George Tyler, 148
Nowell, Charles E., 143

Oliveira Martins, Joaquim Pedro, 63

Parker, Alexander A., 82, 147
Pires de Lima, Joaquim Alberto, 146
Plautus, 146, 150
Pratt, Oscar de, 54, 121
Prestes, António, 149
Primaleón, 100
Psalms, The Book of, 53, 108

Quintela, Paulo, 58

Reckert, Stephen, 23
Reis Brasil, 7
Resende, Garcia de, 19, 20, 26, 27, 28, 76, 77, 112, 118, 119, 120, 134
Révah, I. S., 18, 22, 23, 27, 34, 35, 38, 39, 40, 54, 57, 58, 59, 60, 80, 85, 99
Ribeiro, Bernardim, 133, 134
Ribeiro, Jerónimo, 149
Ribeiro Chiado, António, 142, 148
Rivers, Elias L., 105
Rocha, Andrée Crabbé, 27
Rocha Brito, Alberto da, 79
Rodrigues, Melícia, 21, 81
Rossi, G. C., 58
Ruth, The Book of, 114

Sá de Miranda, Francisco de, 91, 92, 93, 131, 144, 149
Sabugosa, Conde de, 23
San Pedro, Diego de, 84
Sanches de Baena, Visconde de, 17
Sánchez de Badajoz, Garcí, 62
Santillana, Marqués de, 125, 126
Saraiva, António José, 19, 47, 64, 120, 144
Saviotti, Gino, 144
Savonarola, 108, 109
Savoy, Duke of, 20, 76, 127, 134
Sebastião, King, 22
Shakespeare, 7, 42, 51, 84, 125, 149
Spitzer, Leo, 38, 40, 41, 42, 43, 45, 46, 48, 49, 51
Stegagno Picchio, Luciana, 27, 119, 121
Sten, Holger, 145
Stern, Charlotte, 80, 81, 82, 83, 97, 145

Teyssier, Paul, 23, 24, 32, 69, 76
Ticknor, George, 43, 44, 48, 49
Torres Naharro, Bartolomé de, 32, 52, 82, 83

Valdés, Alfonso de, 94
Vega, Lope de, 147, 148, 149
Vicente, Belchior, 21
Vicente, Gil:
  WRITINGS OF:
  (a) Complete Works
    Copilação (1562), 8, 22, 23, 30, 47, 48, 55, 56, 59, 60, 66, 67, 85, 89, 90, 98, 99, 108, 114, 121, 122, 135, 140, 142
    Copilação (1586), 22, 95, 121
  (b) Dramatic Works
    Amadis de Gaula, 8, 85, 98, 99, 102–4, 106–7, 137, 141, 143
    Canaanite Woman, The Play of the, 66, 70–72, 136, 140, 142
    Carriers, The Farce of the, 79, 85, 90–91, 126

[167]

Castilian Pastoral Play, The, 29, 31–32, 34, 36, 53, 136, 138, 141

Coat of Arms of the City of Coimbra, The Play on the, 82, 91, 92–93, 136, 138

Courts of Jupiter, The, 76–77, 111, 127, 133, 134, 137, 139, 142

Doctors, The Play of the, 78–79, 123, 137

Dom Duardos, 8, 80, 82, 84, 85, 98, 99, 100–2, 103, 104–5, 106–7, 117, 120, 127, 138, 139, 141, 142, 147

Exhortation to War, The, 39, 47, 48, 95, 142

Fair, The Play of the, 81, 94–95, 137

Fairies, The Play of the, 72, 75–76, 87, 125, 137

Faith, The Play of, 29, 35, 36–37, 72, 75, 139

Fame, The Play of, 47–48, 136, 139, 142

Festival Play, The, 17, 23, 89–90, 142

Forest of Deceits, The, 21, 73, 88, 97–98, 136, 137, 138, 140, 142

Forge of Love, The, 91–92, 123, 129, 138, 140, 142

Four Seasons, The Play of the, 35, 36, 49–52, 77, 128, 136, 139

Gypsy Women, The Farce of the, 75, 76, 85, 89

Herdsman's Monologue, The, 29, 30, 36, 52, 138

History of God, The Play of the, 66–69, 70, 71, 72, 91, 123, 137, 140, 147

India, The Play of, 26, 29, 36, 59, 73, 74–75, 141

Inês Pereira, The Farce of, 85–86, 88, 89, 109, 141, 148

Judge of Beira, The Farce of the, 85, 87–88, 89, 119, 126, 137

Love's Jubilee [non-extant], 24, 142

Lusitania, The Play of, 79, 96–97, 118, 125, 127, 140, 142

Magi, The Play of the, 29, 33–34, 36, 53, 136, 138, 142

Mofina Mendes, The Play of, 36, 49, 50, 52–53, 82, 121, 128, 136, 139, 143

Old Man of the Orchard, The Farce of the, 79–80, 87, 138

Pastoral Tragicomedy of the Estrêla Mountain Range, The, 91, 93, 124, 129, 135, 136

Pilgrimage of the Aggrieved, The, 79, 97, 98, 114, 119, 128, 138, 142

Portuguese Pastoral Play, The, 32–33, 137, 138

Priest of Beira, The Farce of the, 95–96, 121, 137, 138, 143

Resurrection, The Dialogue on the, 66, 69, 72

Rubena, The Play of, 83–85, 88, 125, 129, 141

St. Martin, The Play of, 29, 34, 68, 142, 148

Ship of Love, The, 91–92, 129, 138, 142

Ships, The (The Ship of Hell, The Ship of Purgatory, The Ship of Heaven), 53, 54–57, 58–59, 61, 62–65, 67, 72, 78, 80, 85, 87, 137, 138, 142, 147, 149

Sibyl Cassandra, The Play of the, 36, 37–46, 47, 48–49, 50, 51, 122, 130, 136, 140, 147

Soul's Journey, The, 53, 54, 57, 59–61, 61–62, 72, 80, 137, 147

Temple of Apollo, The, 88–89, 128, 140

Index

Triumph of Winter, The, 50, 77–78, 124, 126, 128, 129, 139, 142

Visitation, The: See *The Herdsman's Monologue*

Who has Bran?, 29, 36, 73–74, 79, 91, 128, 130, 138, 141, 143, 146

Widower, The Play of the, 80–83, 84, 139

(c) Miscellaneous Works

Complaint, A, 114

Epistle-Dedication to the Copilação, The, 114–15

Epitaph, The Author's, 22

For the Coronation of João III, 112–14

"Have Mercy on Me, O God . . .", 108–9

Letter for Tolerance, A, 69, 115–17

Maria Parda's Lament, 27, 119–21

Prologue-Dedication to Dom Duardos, The, 158

Sermon, The, 109–11, 123

To Afonso Lopes Çapaio, 117–18

To the Conde do Vimioso, 118

To the Memory of Manuel I, 111–12

Vasco Abul's Lawsuit, 118–19

Verses to Felipe Guilhem, 117

Vicente, Luis, 8, 21, 22, 23, 115, 135

Vicente, Paula, 21, 81, 133

Vicente, Valéria, 21

Vicente Anes Joeira, The Play of, 148

Vicente de Burgos, Fray, 51

Virgil, 75

Waldron, T. P., 80, 99, 102, 103, 104, 106

Wardropper, Bruce W., 31, 34, 35, 104, 106, 107

Williams, Ronald B., 31, 136, 137, 138

Young, George, 124, 126, 127, 131

Zamora Vicente, Alonso, 80, 82